THE BRIDGE BUILDER

THE BRIDGE BUILDER

❖

The Life and Continuing Legacy of
Rabbi Yechiel Eckstein

ZEV CHAFETS

SENTINEL

SENTINEL
An imprint of Penguin Random House LLC
375 Hudson Street
New York, New York 10014
penguin.com

Photographs courtesy of the International Fellowship of Christians and Jews

ISBN 978-1-59184-678-9
Printed in the United States of America

1   3   5   7   9   10   8   6   4   2

Set in Janson Text LT Std
Designed by Alissa Rose Theodor

For Alexis Ostrobrod, with love

CONTENTS

❖

Author's Note

❖

The first time I met Yechiel Eckstein, in 2004, I was a columnist at the New York *Daily News*, looking for a story. Someone told me about an Orthodox rabbi out of Chicago who was raising millions for Jewish philanthropy in Israel and the former Soviet Union. This surprised me; in my experience, most rabbis receive charity, not dispense it. Even more surprising—astonishing, in fact—was that these donations were said to come from the evangelical Christians of small-town America, many of whom had never encountered a Jew in person. I was both curious and skeptical.

Eckstein and I met for lunch in New York City, at a kosher pizzeria that he chose. For readers unaccustomed to Jewish dining, suffice it to say that it is almost always a mistake to eat at a place where the kosher certificate in the window is bigger than the menu. This was one of those places.

I should say, right off, that I am not generally an admirer of rabbis. My first brush with one came in Pontiac, Michigan, where I was raised. The Reform rabbi who ministered to our little congregation lived down the street, and my father assigned me the task of mowing his lawn. All I got for the effort was a nod of gratitude. My father explained, ex post facto, that charging a rabbi for labor would be disrespectful. From that day on, I endeavored to be respectful of rabbis from a safe distance.

That became impossible when I moved to Israel at the age of twenty, in 1967. Rabbis were everywhere, and these were the real thing: bearded fundamentalists in black whose worldview and dress code were an unchanging reflection of late medieval Poland. At first, I was charmed by these ancient survivors. That feeling changed to alarm when I realized that they were intent on imposing their absolute rules and retrograde lifestyle on everyone else. Even more alarming, they were organized into political parties that controlled or influenced large swaths of my daily life. Like a great many irreligious Israelis, I became—and have remained—rabbi averse.

As I sat in the kosher pizza parlor, watching Eckstein devour huge slices of double cheese, he didn't really seem like a rabbi to me. Broad-shouldered and big-boned, he was built more like a retired NFL quarterback. He wore a baseball cap instead of a yarmulke and sported a two-day growth of beard, but there was nothing macho about his affect. He was sincere and friendly, devoid of the irony that enlivens so much Jewish conversation. When I remarked on this, he smiled and said, "I'm from Canada."

Eckstein proudly confirmed that the International Fellowship of Christians and Jews—which he referred to as his "ministry"—was raising vast amounts of money from evangelical Christians for Jewish charities. But he wanted me to understand that his "mission" went far beyond that. He was building a bridge between Jews and Christians, who had been divided by animosity and mutual incomprehension for two millennia. He saw himself not as a mere fund-raiser or philanthropist, but as a spiritual teacher, able to show Christians how to reestablish their biblical connection to the Land of Israel and the Jewish people. The money, which he raised mostly by direct mail and infomercials in which he starred, was a by-product.

Naturally, I was suspicious. After the Jim Bakker and Jimmy Swaggart scandals, televangelists had a bad reputation. And it was extremely unusual to hear an Orthodox rabbi talk about Christianity in any but a disparaging way. But Eckstein checked out. He had a prestigious rabbinical degree. And there really was a Fellowship doing what he said it did. I looked for scandals and found none, and eventually wrote a nice little man-bites-dog story.

A couple of years later, I wrote a full-length profile of Eckstein for the *New York Times Magazine.* I went out to Chicago and inspected the premises, saw him in action on the pulpit of a Pentecostal church in Indiana, interviewed his staff, friends, and enemies, and wrote a piece called "The Rabbi Who Loved Evangelicals (and Vice Versa)" in which I referred to him as the rabbi with the biggest Gentile following since Jesus. The piece was respectful, but I was not completely sold. If you go to the Yechiel Eckstein Wikipedia page, you'll see that most of the material in the "criticism" section stems from what I wrote.

By now, the subject of evangelical-Jewish relations fascinated me, and in 2007, I published a book titled *A Match Made in Heaven.*

Eckstein served as my guide to what was (and remains) mostly un-charted territory. He took me with him to a meeting with Jerry Falwell at Liberty University in Lynchburg, Virginia; walked me through a Christian Booksellers Convention in Denver; and allowed me to come along as he led a group of evangelicals on a ten-day pilgrimage to Israel. Over the years we met often in New York and at his Chicago headquarters, where he let me see for myself how the philanthropic sausage was made.

During these years, Eckstein's Fellowship grew into the largest private charitable foundation in Israel as well as the underwriter of much of the Jewish life of Eastern Europe. As an adopted Israeli, I appreciated what he was doing. He was also fun to hang around with, full of energy and enthusiasm rare in a man his age (or mine). Over time we became friends.

Occasionally we discussed the idea of my writing a book about his life and times. I was tempted. My last two books were biographies of Rush Limbaugh and Roger Ailes, the founder of Fox News. Like them, Eckstein is a brilliant communicator, a self-made entrepreneur, and a man willing to stand up for his ideas in the face of vitriolic opposition from the establishment (in Eckstein's case, several estab-lishments). They all changed conventional wisdom about what was possible. I had no doubt that a book about Yechiel's life was an in-teresting and worthwhile project, but I was reluctant to do it myself.

I hope I don't shock you with the revelation that there is no such thing as objective biography. Nor is it unheard-of for authors to write about personal friends. But it has some obvious dangers, and some less obvious. Offending a friend in print is a good way to put a dent in the friendship. Yet self-censorship guarantees a dull book at best and—unless readers know exactly what you are doing—a dishonest one.

So let me be clear. This book is authorized. My advance against royalties is partly underwritten by the IFCJ. My royalties will go to the IFCJ. This is Rabbi Eckstein's story, and much of it is told in his words. But that is not the same as saying that this is an "as-told-to" book. I am confident of the essential facts of the narrative because I have covered Rabbi Eckstein and his ministry for more than a decade. If there were skeletons, I would, I think, know about them. Yechiel is not a man who keeps secrets.

As I worked on the book, a writer friend read it over my shoulder, and peppered me with comments like "This will never stay in" or "No way he's going to let you write that," or just "You must be kidding!" When Yechiel went over the finished product, he asked me to remove exactly *one* thing—an unflattering remark he made about a relative. His comments were mostly attempts to explain the spiritual dimension of his activities, which I often didn't quite grasp. Not only did he accept unflattering descriptions of his character, behavior, and motivations, he actually added examples. If you think I'm making this up, read the book and decide for yourself.

Still, I can't say that this book is unbiased. I went into it liking and admiring Yechiel Eckstein. After countless hours with him, I like and admire him more. I have seen for myself the good he does with the money he has raised. I have watched him wrestle with his enemies, his critics, and most of all, his own personal doubts and demons. I have even, on occasion, been vicariously moved by his spirituality.

I still don't really have a rabbi. I'm not the type, I guess. But if I did, he's the one I would want.

THE BRIDGE BUILDER

One

❖

"THE WORST DAY OF MY LIFE"

On a bleak Chicago Saturday in the winter of 1989, Rabbi Yechiel Eckstein and his wife, Bonnie, rose early and put on their Sabbath finery. That morning their firstborn, Tamar, was to celebrate her bat mitzvah, the coming-of-age party that marks the twelfth birthday of Orthodox Jewish girls.

The Ecksteins had come to Chicago from New York eleven years earlier, after he finished rabbinical school at Yeshiva University and she completed her BA at Barnard College. For the first six years, he worked in the local office of the Anti-Defamation League (ADL), promoting interfaith activism on First Amendment issues. In 1983, he left to found his own organization, the Holyland Fellowship of Christians and Jews. The Christians with whom he fostered friendship were not the usual mainline liberal Protestants and Catholic dignitaries with whom the heads of American Jewry were friendly. They were evangelicals:

1

born-again, Bible-loving Christians of a kind that most Jews rarely encountered. To the extent they were thought of at all, it was as the Other—a pack of Bible-thumping racists and Jew haters from the hinterlands. But Yechiel had learned to see past the stereotype. The evangelicals he came across in the Midwest were everyday Americans whose religious beliefs made them eager to meet and befriend the Jews, God's chosen people. He saw the potential for a great Judeo-Christian alliance that would serve as a force for Israel and Jewish causes around the world, and help America stay on a moral course at home. It was a vision shared by virtually no one else in the Jewish community, but he pursued it with single-minded energy. To make ends meet, he held down weekend pulpits in small Orthodox congregations around the city, performed concerts, and sang at weddings with a band he put together.

In the Chicago newspapers, articles described Eckstein's work for the ADL—teaching a course in Judaism sponsored by the Roman Catholic archdiocesan school board, leading sessions for Christian doctrine teachers on "the Jewish roots of Christianity," addressing a conference of priests and nuns on "how God speaks to us." One story noted that he had put together perhaps the world's first Jewish-evangelical conference. Still, he was far from being famous, and now that he was out on his own, leading his own ministry, he worked hard to garner the attention needed to expand.

Bonnie, his wife, saw this work as evidence of emotional neediness, and she didn't like it. She had fallen in love with a rabbi's son, a big, good-natured jock who had played basketball for the Yeshiva University High School team and performed Hebrew folk music for adoring audiences on the kosher college music circuit. Now he seemed different, a driven and exhausted man with a dream she neither understood nor shared. Bonnie had nothing against Christians. She had known some at Barnard. It was the *sort* of Christians Yechiel was working with, and sometimes dragging home for Sabbath dinner—*Republican* Christians, Reaganites, full of Jesus talk and pious curiosity about the Shabbat rituals. Yechiel, thank God, was still a Democrat, but he was also a friend of Pat Robertson's—had actually appeared on his TV show, *The 700 Club.* No one she knew watched, but still . . .

Family tensions were put aside that Shabbat morning, as they headed for the small Chabad *shul* in a strip mall near their home in Skokie. Yechiel's downtown synagogue was too far for their friends and neighbors to reach on foot (Orthodox Jews are not allowed to travel by car on the Sabbath) and, in any case, he didn't want a repetition of his own bar mitzvah, when the stress of performing in front of his father's congregation gave him an unstoppable nosebleed that forced him to scratch his sermonic "*D'var Torah*" speech. Tamar wouldn't be commenting on the weekly Torah portion during the service—Orthodox girls don't do that—but she would be the belle of the morning, asked to speak at the party afterward. Yechiel wanted to make sure that she would be relaxed and happy. She and Bonnie had decorated the small social hall with blue and white balloons and replaced the stained white tablecloths with festive blue ones. A large cake inscribed with the words "Mazel Tov Tamar" was placed at the head table.

As Bonnie and Tamar surveyed their handiwork, a severe-looking young rabbi appeared, gave the decorations a disapproving once-over, and informed them that balloons were not allowed in his synagogue, a heretofore unknown prohibition. He also ordered them to remove the new tablecloths and replace them with the old ones. And, after inspecting the cake, he ruled that it was not kosher: it was forbidden to cut letters of the alphabet on the Sabbath. Yechiel was upstairs at the time, taking part in Shabbat prayers. He knew nothing about the rabbi's hostile attitude, or the pressure it had put on his wife and eldest daughter.

After the Torah reading, Yechiel was planning on leading the prayers. It was the usual thing, especially for a father who was also a rabbi and a cantor. He went to the lectern and began with the opening prayer. Then the young rabbi came up and said, "No, no, no." Yechiel was confused, but he stepped away from the pulpit. "I knew I was a controversial person, but I had been praying in that Chabad shul for a long time and at first I was shocked to be turned away like that."

The small shul was filled that day with friends, virtually all of them Orthodox Jews. Silently he walked to the back, covered his head in his prayer shawl, and sat there, half listening, praying that his daughter's special day hadn't been ruined. "I was mortified." Still, he understood. He knew that Halacha (Orthodox rabbinical law) prohibited Jews from entering Christian churches. It was considered *avoda zara*, idol worship, to teach Torah to Gentiles—a crime he committed every time he preached to an evangelical congregation about the blessings God had promised those who bless the Jews, or quoted the Zionist prophecies of Isaiah and Jeremiah. Senior rabbis at his alma mater, Yeshiva University, had denounced him. His own father disapproved of what he was doing. Orthodox Judaism is about maintaining borders between the

Jewish people and the Gentile world, and Eckstein had transgressed those borders.

And yet, huddled under his prayer shawl, Yechiel Eckstein felt something else: a sense of defiance. He was a seeker and a self-examiner, a chronic critic of his own motives. But at this moment he trusted his vision. A bridge uniting Christians and Jews could be built, and he felt destined to be the engineer. He had no idea how hard the work would be, the price it would exact. He only knew, with a certainty he had never before felt, that he had no choice but to go ahead.

More than thirty years later, Eckstein recalls that certainty. "I felt humiliated and alone. It was the worst day of my life. But I never thought I was wrong. It didn't even occur to me to quit. I have a personal relationship with God and I felt at the time that it was a divine mission, what is known in Hebrew as *shlichut*. Sitting in the back of the shul that day, I thought about Abraham and Isaac. In the book of Genesis, God commands Abraham to take his son 'to the land I will show you.' He doesn't tell Abraham where it is. He simply expects Abraham to obey. I had a moral certainty that came from God. And I still feel it. That's what has guided my work and my life, from the beginning until today."

Two

❖

CORNERSTONE

Being called out as a bad Jew during your daughter's bat mitzvah would be a memorably awful experience for any father. It was especially traumatic for Eckstein, the scion of a family whose tradition of piety and community leadership went back centuries and spanned continents. The family name can be traced back to the time of the Austro-Hungarian Empire. Until 1787, the Jews there were known to one another, and the authorities, only by a Hebrew first name and the first name of their father; but that year, an edict of Emperor Joseph II required all his Jewish male subjects to choose a Germanic family name or have one chosen for them by a government official. Many picked colors—Roth (red), Weiss (white), Schwartz (black); occupations—Kaufman (merchant), Kravitz (tailor); or their towns of origin. Yechiel's ancestors chose Eckstein, which means "cornerstone," a name that reflected their view of their place in the community. For generations, the clan had produced rabbis and religious judges, ritual slaughterers and *mohels* (ritual circumcisers), synagogue cantors and *balebatishe lamdanim*, scholarly laymen. Eckstein men married the daughters of similarly esteemed figures. "Cornerstone" was a proud name, but not an inaccurate one; families such as this helped bind together the sometimes nomadic and often embattled Jews of Middle Europe.

The position of Hungary's Jews slowly improved during the nineteenth century. In the Revolutions of 1848, Jews fought side by side with Hungarians, and in 1867 they were granted full citizenship. For the first time they were free to leave their towns and villages and to live and work as they chose. Ambitious young men made their way to Budapest, enrolled in universities, and pursued professions. Some became socialists. Others were attracted to the radically liberal Reform Judaism that was newly imported from Germany. A small but increasing number converted to Christianity. Everything seemed possible. The most intrepid souls set out for foreign destinations—the great cities of Western Europe and the golden streets of America.

Simcha Bunam Eckstein, a prosperous young businessman from the town of Weitzen, joined the exodus in 1867. But his destination wasn't Budapest or New York. Instead, he and his wife, Yutel, traveled east to Jerusalem, the ancient Jewish capital, which had been ruled by a succession of Roman and Christian emperors before falling to the Ottoman Turks. As part of the Ottoman Empire, the fabled city was little more than a dusty provincial town of about fifteen thousand people, a third of them Jews. Political Zionism was still a gleam in Theodor Herzl's eye, but Jewish Jerusalemites like Simcha Bunam weren't Zionists. They were religious pietists—Sephardim who had returned to the Holy Land from exile in Islamic countries; Hasidim from Europe who practiced a fervent style of worship; and more traditional Orthodox Jews. Whatever their differences, they shared a belief that a Third Temple would be established in Jerusalem only when God was ready and only through his agency.

Simcha Bunam Eckstein bought a small home in a new neighborhood within walking distance of the Temple Mount, now under the sultan's control. The neighborhood, called Kollel Shomrei Hahomot (Guardians of the Walls), was built by fellow Hungarian Jews. He and Yutel were childless, but they raised three orphan children—two girls and a boy, the son of Simcha's dead brother Yechzkel. The boy's name was Yechiel Zvi Eckstein.

The young Eckstein had a typical religious education, meaning that he received almost nothing in the way of secular learning. Most of the Jews in the Holy Land spent their time studying Talmud. Work was the exception; people were sustained by alms and contributions from abroad. When Yechiel Zvi came of age, he married a young woman, Gitel Preuiss, whose father, recently arrived from Hungary, was a cloistered mystic. The elder Preuiss's days were spent in the synagogue declaiming "Time is short and the work is great!" and his nights were given over to the study of kabbalah with a rabbi from Yemen—behavior that was considered extreme even among the God-struck pietists of the Jewish community of Jerusalem.

That community occupied a place of precipitous change. In World War I, the British captured Jerusalem from the Ottoman Empire, and established sovereignty there. In November 1917, British foreign minister Arthur Balfour sent a letter to Baron Walter Rothschild, the leader of British Jewry, promising support for a Jewish homeland in Palestine. The letter, known as the Balfour Declaration, recognized the extraordinary momentum Zionism had gained since the first secular Jewish pioneers arrived in the Holy Land in 1880. The modern Zionist movement was barely twenty years old, but it had captured the imagination of Jews around the world. Young socialist idealists came to create communal farms in the Galilee, seeking "to build and be rebuilt" in the soil of their ancient homeland. At the time, there were about forty thousand of these pioneers in the country. The ultra-Orthodox had little to do with them; for the pietists, these new settlers were heretics who profaned Hebrew by using it in daily speech and who sought, through their activism, to replace God's timetable with their own. Jews like the Ecksteins felt no need to be "rebuilt" by physical labor or self-defense. They were content to live as their ancestors had, honoring tradition and observing the laws and practices of the Torah.

In the decade after the Balfour Declaration, the pioneer population nearly quadrupled, to almost 150,000. This alarmed the Arab population, which had its own postwar aspirations. In April 1920, the pious Jews of Jerusalem were set upon by mobs incited by local Islamic leaders. A few of the men tried feebly to defend themselves with rocks and boiling water, but they really had no idea how to fight. The rioting lasted three days and ended only when British troops stepped in and declared martial law. By then, five of the city's Jews had been murdered and more than two hundred injured.

Yechiel Zvi Eckstein and his family couldn't have known that this was a prelude to a battle for the Holy City that is now in its tenth decade. What they did know was that Jerusalem had become an inhospitable and possibly dangerous place. In 1928, they decided they had had enough and decamped for the United States. On the boat to America, Yechiel Zvi cut off the side curls of his nine-year-old grandson Shimon, who would henceforth be known as Simon, or Sy. It was a gesture of assimilation, a sign that the ultra-Orthodox family was willing to make at least a cosmetic effort to fit into their new country.

In America, Yechiel Zvi found work in Little Rock, Arkansas, where Jewish peddlers and merchants had established a small community. His business card announced the arrival in Dixie of "Rabbi Y. Z. Eckstein, Practical Mohel, and Wedding Ceremonies Performed." Gitel took a look around, pronounced the place unfit for Jews, and left, to make her way back to Jerusalem. Yechiel Zvi, for reasons known primarily to himself, stayed on, with his son and grandchildren; it took him eleven years to rejoin his wife in the little house not far from the Wailing Wall.

Sy Eckstein, despite his Grandmother Gitel's concerns about the viability of Jewish survival in America, grew into a talented Talmud student and a precocious synagogue singer and choir director. Only a year before the Ecksteins arrived in America, Al Jolson had starred in the first talkie, *The Jazz Singer*, a film about a gifted singer, the son of a rabbi, who left the fold for the allure of show business. But young Sy wasn't a jazz singer. He was an Eckstein, a cornerstone of the Jewish community, no more drawn to the lights of Broadway than his ancestor Simcha Bunam had been by the pleasures of secular Budapest. He finished high school and enrolled in Yeshiva University in New York City, where he was eventually ordained as a rabbi. While he was there, he met his future wife, Belle, at a dance sponsored by Young Israel. It was a daring thing to do—previous generations of Ecksteins had found their brides through carefully arranged marriages—but Sy and Belle belonged to the "modern Orthodox" world, an American attempt to fuse strict adherence to the Torah with an embrace of scientific knowledge and contemporary culture.

After being ordained, Sy took a job as the assistant rabbi at the Jewish Center on West Eighty-Sixth Street, one of the most prominent modern Orthodox synagogues in America. From there he went to Winthrop, Massachusetts, a heavily Jewish suburb of Boston, as head rabbi. A pair of notable events marked his three-year tenure in Winthrop. His eldest son was born, in 1951, and named Yechiel Zvi, after his deceased great-grandfather. (As was the custom, Yechiel also received an "American" name—Joel Harris Eckstein—although nobody ever really called him that.) The other extraordinary moment came when Sy saved the life of a drowning man at a local beach. In landlocked Jerusalem, the city of his birth, Jews generally didn't know how to swim, and even in America, Orthodox rabbis were rarely found at the beach. The story became a part of Eckstein family lore.

Then and now, young rabbis building a career tend to move around a lot, and in 1952 the Ecksteins departed for Ottawa. The Canadian capital had a few hundred Jewish families divided among four synagogues. Over a few years, Sy Eckstein consolidated them into one congregation, Beth Shalom. Many of the members were only nominally Orthodox, but Rabbi Eckstein decided it was better to include everyone, even at the cost of compromise. So if his congregants drove to the synagogue on Saturday in violation of Sabbath rules, or disobeyed kashrut (Orthodox dietary laws), he turned a blind eye. Such flexibility won him a reputation as a liberal and welcoming rabbi. But he was strict in his own observance. There was only one other home in Ottawa where the food was deemed kosher enough for the Eckstein children to eat. When Yechiel visited his other playmates, Gentile or Jewish, he brought his own refreshments.

On the pulpit, Rabbi Eckstein cut a commanding figure. He was well over six feet tall, his height accentuated by a formal silk top hat. He was a stickler for decorum, not a notable quality of most Orthodox shuls. At Beth Shalom, good manners and the right appearance mattered. "It was a very proper, somewhat pompous place with a sort of British atmosphere," recalls Yechiel. "I remember as a young boy watching my father standing on the bimah [the platform around the altar] in his black robe, in a very formal pose. He could be very intimidating." As the rabbi of the Canadian capital, he was invited to represent the Jewish community on state occasions, such as visits by Queen Elizabeth and other British royals, and at the annual opening session of Parliament. He also participated in brotherhood events on behalf of the Ottawa Jewish community.

Sy relished his ecumenical public role, but the ecumenism was superficial. Like most Jews of the time and place, he and his wife very rarely socialized with Gentiles. A Catholic church stood next door to the synagogue parsonage where they lived, but the Eckstein kids were forbidden to enter—and in any case Yechiel doesn't remember being especially interested in what went on inside. Yechiel had only a few Christian friends, neighborhood kids with whom he played ball. One of them, Brian Hawlee, became a priest. There must have been evangelical Christians in Ottawa, but they didn't get invited to state dinners or parliamentary openings, and Sy and Belle and their children probably never ran into any of them.

The Eckstein marriage was a love match that lasted; in 2014 they celebrated their fifty-eighth anniversary. To their children they often seemed like a closed partnership. Rabbi Eckstein was an aloof and sometimes harsh father, Belle an elegant consort and helpmate and a dutiful but distant mother. Thinking back, Yechiel can't recall a single time either of his parents hugged him or told him they loved him. "We kids were irrelevant," he says. Husband and wife dined alone, after the children had been fed and sent upstairs. A family joke was that Rabbi Eckstein called home each evening from his office to make sure the kids were already out of the way. "As they got older, my parents grew more mellow and loving," Eckstein says. "My siblings and I can only smile at how giving and attentive they have become toward us and especially their grandchildren."

The absence of money was a constant in the Eckstein family. "I desperately wanted a football helmet like the other kids. I begged for one. Finally my father bought me a helmet—made of *cardboard*. I begged for a bike too. My father eventually brought one home. It was used. And it was a girls' model." Sy and Belle maintained a front of grand style, but Yechiel knew it was a facade. He was humiliated when he was periodically called down to the principal's office and reprimanded because his father had missed a tuition payment. And he was mortified to overhear his mother begging her husband to ask the president of the congregation for money to replace the threadbare carpet in the parsonage.

Sy and Belle entertained their friends graciously, but their kids didn't get any of the goodies that were served. As a small boy, Yechiel was so hungry for sweets that he drank an entire bottle of honey-flavored cough syrup and had to be rushed to the hospital to have his stomach pumped. When he was caught trying to sneak cookies, or violating other house rules, he was punished, sometimes severely. His parents believed in the Talmudic injunction that a man who refrains from chastising his son shows hatred for the boy.

The one break in the routine was the Sabbath meal that followed services. Sabbath songs were sung, in accordance with tradition, and occasionally Rabbi Eckstein even joshed with the kids. Sometimes Yechiel was allowed to invite a friend—Jimmy Shalom, who lived nearby, or Mel Rosenberg, a classmate at Hillel Academy. After the final benediction, Eckstein's parents adjourned to their second-floor bedroom for a nap. After they were safely asleep, the boys played soccer in the downstairs hallway. When the hall got too dark to see the ball, Mel and Yechiel decided that while turning on the lights with their hands was forbidden ("probably punishable by death" Rosenberg wrote more than fifty years later) there was no biblical prohibition against using their teeth. They used the same method to turn on the television to watch Ottawa Rough Riders football games. Changing channels was difficult, but Yechiel mastered it "one click at a time."

Yechiel was a standout athlete at Hillel Academy, bigger and more athletic than the other boys. "During the winter, we would play football during recess," Rosenberg recalls. "On one occasion, Yechiel had caught the ball and was on his way to a decisive touchdown. I was the lone defender. I lunged at his feet as he confidently ran around me and managed to trip him up in the snow. Tackling Yechiel was such a rare and exceptional incident that I remember this brief moment of childhood glory to this day." Eckstein does too. "To be honest, it was embarrassing to be tackled by Mel," he recalls.

Yechiel Eckstein may have been a schoolboy hero, but he harbored deep doubts about himself. When he was nine, he and a friend, Frankie Rosen, walked past the swimming pool outside the Jewish community center and saw a body lying at the bottom. Rosen, acting instinctively, tried to scale the fence to reach the drowned body. Yechiel stood frozen. He didn't even shout for help. The body was already dead; there was nothing that either boy could have done. But Yechiel couldn't help contrasting his hesitance with his father's quick action at the beach in Massachusetts. He felt that he didn't measure up, a feeling Sy Eckstein did nothing to dispel.

"My father never believed in me, and he let me know it," says Eckstein. "He thought everything I said was foolish. The Rough

Riders had a quarterback I looked up to, Russ Jackson. Whenever I came up with an idea, my father would dismiss it as a stupid fantasy. 'Jackson to Eckstein for the winning touchdown,' he'd say in a sarcastic, mocking tone. 'Like you're really going to save the game.'"

Despite Yechiel's resentments, he kept up a facade. "Honor your father and mother" was an injunction he took seriously, and he didn't want to do anything that might harm his father's image. Yechiel quickly developed a performer's ability to fake his moods. "I knew how to show people what they want to see," he says. "I figured out how to turn it on and off." For many years, he starred in the role of the dutiful son of the Canadian capital's First Jewish Family.

From the age of seven, Yechiel and his elder sister Rachel (known as Rock), his younger sister, Ahuva, and eventually, his baby brother Berl were sent to Morasha, a modern Orthodox summer camp in the Poconos. He and Ahuva—remembered by her fellow campers for her vivacious personality and good looks—entertained the other kids by singing duets of Hebrew pop songs and Canadian folk tunes. Once again, Yechiel was a star and, although he was lonely, he didn't really mind being away from home.

There weren't enough Orthodox Jewish children in Ottawa to support a religious high school, and so Yechiel and a few other local boys were sent to New York, where they could get a proper yeshiva education. Girls were supposed to stay home and attend public school, but Ahuva rebelled, and after a struggle she was allowed to go to New York, where she boarded with an observant family and studied at the Hebrew Institute of Long Island. After his bar mitzvah, Yechiel followed. The bar mitzvah itself had been a bloody-nosed fiasco, and his misery was compounded when his parents seized his gift money to pay for the party.

From the time he left home at thirteen, Yechiel saw his mother and father two or three times a year, rarely for more than a few days. Every Friday before sunset, he dutifully called home to wish them a good Shabbat, but it was clear to him that he was basically on his own, especially after Ahuva left to study in Israel. At fourteen, he transferred to Yeshiva University High School and lived in the dorm in Washington Heights. It has since come out, most recently in a class-action lawsuit, that there were sexual predators among the faculty, known to touch the boys under the pretext of making sure they were wearing their *tzitzes* (fringes of the ritual undershirt worn by Orthodox Jewish men). A number of times Yechiel found himself cornered by a rabbi who came too close for comfort. But he didn't complain; nobody complained back then, and in any case there was no one to complain to.

Orthodox Judaism of the Yeshiva University High variety did not place a high premium on spirituality. Prayer was a thrice-daily routine, an obligation, a set of words to be memorized and declaimed in their proper order. Yechiel wanted more; he sought a personal connection with God in his *davening* (the Yiddish term for praying). "I desperately strove for *devekut*, literally a union with God, that would bring spiritual euphoria. I prayed so hard for it that when I couldn't get there, I became depressed."

Some of his classmates and not a few of his teachers saw his conspicuously emotional style of prayer as an affectation. His father felt the same way. Once, during a school vacation in Ottawa, Yechiel remained standing, lost in prayer, while the other members of his father's congregation were seated. This violation of ritual decorum brought him a parental reprimand as well as some personal discomfort. "I never liked attracting attention to myself," he recalls. "But at the yeshiva in New York we stood for the Kaddish prayer, so I stood in my father's shul. Being different from all the others made me cringe. But at the same time I felt grown up, like a real yeshiva student, and I wanted people to know it."

As a teenager, Yechiel had two extracurricular passions: music and sports. He was a self-taught guitar player and singer, a folkie who loved Peter, Paul and Mary and idolized Rabbi Shlomo Carlebach, the itinerant spiritual guru, composer of sacred music, and dynamic performer who was later immortalized in the Broadway show *Soul Doctor.* As a basketball player, Yechiel was a six-foot-two forward, a rugged rebounder with a sweet eighteen-foot jump shot.

All this contributed to Yechiel's reputation among his friends as a ladies' man. Yeshiva High School was not coed, but when Eckstein managed to get around girls, his behavior was considered racy by the prim standards of his world. He was once suspended from school for talking to a girl on the phone. At camp, where the sexes had separate beaches, he got in trouble for leaning out a bus window and wolf-whistling at a group of girls in bathing suits. Still, he dated only Orthodox *frum* girls from good Orthodox families, and the encounters were innocent—he may have reached first base but, according to him, he never tried to steal second.

As a sophomore, he played basketball for the Yeshiva High School team, and he expected to start in his junior year. But that summer the entire squad went to Camp Raleigh, a kosher camp that emphasized sports, where they honed their game and blended as a unit. Yechiel begged to join them, but his father insisted that he return to the more religious Camp Morasha. "I tried to explain to my father that not going with the rest of the team would hurt my chances of starting, but he didn't care what I wanted. Basketball meant nothing to him, and my desires weren't important. He decided and that was that. To this day I'm still irked by it," says Eckstein.

The season opened with Yechiel, as he predicted, sitting on the bench. He also didn't endear himself by insisting, in an article in the school newspaper, that the players wear their yarmulkes on the court, as he did. "We played in Madison Square Garden twice—once in the old Garden, once in the new—and I opened the game on the bench both times. I knew I was good enough to start. Twice during high school I replaced a sick kid in the starting lineup and I was high scorer each time. It was humiliating being on the sidelines, especially with all the girls watching."

During high school, Yechiel began to experience periods of withdrawal, when he'd sit alone in his room playing guitar or just staring at the ceiling. "I had the sense that I was falling into a deep, black hole with no one to help me climb out," he recalls. "It was frightening, but

I really had no one to turn to." There were no school psychologists at Yeshiva University High School, no one to tell him that he was depressed. At camp, he discussed his existential angst and mood swings with Rabbi Norman Lamm, whom he considered a father figure. Lamm, who later became the head of Yeshiva University, told him not to worry. After all, the famed Kotzker Rebbe—a nineteenth-century Hasidic mystic—had suffered from a similar cycle of highs and lows; perhaps it was a sign of greatness. This was more encouragement than Yechiel was used to receiving, and he began studying the writings of the Kotzker Rebbe, whose teachings included observations such as "If I am I because I am I, and you are you because you are you, then I am I and you are you. But if I am I because you are you and you are you because I am I, then I am not I and you are not you!" Not surprisingly, the teenager didn't find much therapeutic value in such musings.

Three

❖

REBEL IN A SKULLCAP

After graduating, in 1968, Yechiel spent two years in Kerem B'Yavneh, a yeshiva in Israel. "In my milieu it was a normal thing to do, the path that had been set for me by my parents and my schooling," he says. "If I had thought about it I suppose I would have said I was going to eventually become a rabbi, but I don't remember thinking much about the future. I just thought a yeshiva in Israel was the next logical step in the progression of my life, so I went."

He found the regimen brutally difficult—rising before dawn, breakfasting on bread and hard-boiled eggs, and then studying the Talmud from 6:00 a.m. until nearly midnight, with brief breaks for spartan meals and a short nap after lunch. Always a voracious eater, he suffered constantly from hunger pangs. "Once a week they served us a chicken leg for lunch, along with rice and bread and beets. I used to mix them together to make it seem like more," he recalls.

On Fridays, when there were no classes, he walked through the cotton fields to a greasy spoon in the nearest town, where he wolfed down shish kebabs wrapped in pita.

Yechiel wasn't a great Talmud student at Kerem B'Yavneh, but he was the class expert on Jewish philosophy. The subject was divided into two basic categories, *musar* (morality) and *machshava* (thought), and he favored the latter, with its gentler message of human frailty. "Musar books tell you what you can't do and why it is a sin," he says. "Machshava books teach that you have free will, including the freedom to sin. You shouldn't put yourself in compromising positions, but God forgives weakness."

Some of the students were Israelis who were doing military service along with their studies, or veterans who still served in the reserves. It was difficult to connect with them; they were older, and their rough sabra manners tended to be off-putting. The yeshiva considered sports frivolous. There were no girls around, and no social life to speak of. Yechiel had a large extended family in the ultra-Orthodox neighborhoods of Jerusalem, but they were more than an hour away, and most of them didn't have phones; they were throwbacks, not much different from the Jews of Simcha Bunam's day. He visited his aunts and uncles from time to time, but while he was warmly received, they didn't have much to say to one another.

As Yechiel settled into yeshiva life, he was often troubled, and sometimes barely able to function. Israel in those days was not a society that indulged emotional issues. The country was full of survivors: Holocaust victims, displaced Jews from the Arab world, war widows, soldiers, and people living in Third World poverty. "Suck it up" was a national motto. The only kindred soul he found was an eccentric rabbi and spiritual adviser, Rabbi David Lifshitz, who had studied clinical psychology and was willing to listen sympathetically to the woes of a lonely eighteen-year-old American. "He was an interesting guy," Eckstein remembers, "mystical and offbeat, especially for a yeshiva rabbi. He used to do graphology. Boys who were thinking of getting married would bring him samples of a girl's handwriting and he would tell them if it was a good match."

Rabbi Lifshitz became Eckstein's confidant. "He was the first person who gave me time, who recognized my depression and essentially told me that it is okay to feel that way." He also helped Yechiel cope with one of his greatest adolescent anxieties. "Rabbi Lifshitz was the first person I ever told that I had sexual fantasies. In Jewish law it says that someone who spills his own seed is destroying a human life. I felt tremendous guilt over doing it, really horrible. He helped me get over that. He was a genuinely cathartic figure for me."

The long hours of study and isolation had a strong impact on Yechiel. Always religiously observant, he became more meticulous in his prayers and dress. Modern Orthodox men—at Yeshiva High School in New York and on religious kibbutzim in Israel—wore small knitted skullcaps and dressed in a secular style. Yechiel began to wear a black fedora, an emblem of ultra-Orthodoxy, and to let the fringes of his *tzitzes*, which he had always tucked into his trousers, dangle at his sides. These were the external signs of an inner search for meaning and a connection with God that seemed to be absent from the legalistic Talmudic texts, the rote prayers, and the stoicism of his fellow students. When he came back from Israel on vacation, he astonished his family with his clothing and manner. He wouldn't shake women's hands, and he even refused to hug his aunt. Like standing in his father's synagogue while others prayed seated, Yechiel thought his new dress and behavior were appropriate for an advanced yeshiva scholar, but it proved to be a passing phase. "The new, austere me just wasn't me," he says. By the time he returned to the yeshiva, he was his old knit-yarmulke, jeans-wearing, aunt-hugging self.

Israel in those days was still euphoric over its victory in the Six-Day War. In the modern Orthodox yeshiva world, patriotic pride was compounded by a sense that the reuniting of Jerusalem and the capture of the Temple Mount were signs that God was—after an inexplicable absence during the Holocaust—once again working in Jewish history. Some believed that the Messiah might be at hand. In Yechiel's eyes, the soldiers he was studying with were guardians of the nation, avengers of the crimes of the Nazis, instruments of God's purpose—and, of course, irresistibly cool. Israel was fighting a war of attrition against Egypt in Sinai, and he would watch the Israelis heading to the front with Uzis and Kalashnikov rifles slung over their shoulders. It made him recall the words Moses had used to rebuke the tribes of Israel that didn't want to participate in the conquest of the Promised Land: "Should your fellow Israelites go to war while you sit here?" The phrase ran through his mind again and again. One day, after watching soldiers return from an especially dangerous mission, he placed a long-distance call to Ottawa and informed his parents that he had decided to join the paratroopers.

All his life, Yechiel had learned Zionism from his parents. Sy was an enthusiastic fund-raiser and an ardent preacher of Jewish nationalism. After one of his visits to Israel he delivered a memorable sermon on the "glorious mood of dedicated co-responsibility" that all Jews should feel toward the new nation. "We feel the glow of an inner compulsion to do all we can to help our brothers," he said.

Now Yechiel was ready to act on his own inner compulsion to serve. But for Sy Eckstein, sermons were one thing, the future of his elder son something entirely different. He and Belle informed Yechiel that he was still only a boy. They wouldn't allow him to indulge in any Jackson-to-Eckstein foolishness about joining the army. "When I told my parents I wanted to stay and serve, that I felt a sense of personal responsibility to defend the country, they scoffed. 'What difference can *you* make?' my father asked." The decision was final: Yechiel would come back to the United States and attend Yeshiva University. Such high-handedness would have been annoying to a young man in any circumstances; for Yechiel, it was especially galling because, when he turned eighteen, his parents had informed him that he was being "checked off" their list of responsibilities. He would have to go to college, yes. But he would have to pay for it by himself.

Yechiel wasn't a rebel, at least not yet, and he was torn between his sense of duty to Israel and his obligation to honor his father and mother. Since these were both religious commandments, he decided to seek a rabbinical opinion. Searching for an unquestionable source of authority, he rode the bus to Jerusalem, walked to the Mercaz Ha'Rav Yeshiva—the epicenter of the messianic, post–Six-Day War fervor—and requested a meeting with Rabbi Zvi Yehuda Kook.

Rabbi Kook was the legendary head of Mercaz Ha'Rav Yeshiva, the unquestioned spiritual leader of the settlement movement that burgeoned on the West Bank of the Jordan River after the Six-Day War. At the age of eighty-one, he was not the sort of personage an unannounced and unknown American teenager might normally drop in on. Yechiel's meeting was arranged by two students he knew at Mercaz Ha'Rav, who asked Rabbi Kook to see him. "He was a short man with a white beard, hunched over and frail," says Yechiel. "We met in his study on the second floor. Of course, I had heard all kinds of things about him, but he really didn't seem very charismatic or dynamic, and he certainly didn't seem very interested in me or my problems. The whole thing took about five minutes." Kook cited a Talmudic edict that honoring one's father and mother was an important commandment but not obligatory if the parents give the child an order that contradicts a more important mitzvah—in this case the commandment to settle and defend the Land of Israel.

Yechiel thanked Rabbi Kook for his time and wisdom, returned to the Yeshiva, called his parents—and told them he had decided to do as they said and return to New York. The decision had less to do with filial obedience than with his uncertainty about leaving America for good and becoming an Israeli. And, like any young man, he faced the idea of military service with personal doubts—what if he didn't turn out to be paratrooper material? He had stood helpless at the fence as Frankie Rosen desperately tried to raise a drowned body from the bottom of a swimming pool; he might freeze again in an emergency. Yechiel came back to New York and enrolled in Yeshiva University, but the decision not to enlist bothered him. "I felt shamed by it," he says. "But I wasn't a Zionist in the same sense as the settlers in the West Bank are. I wasn't ideologically driven in that way." He told himself that his decision to come back to the States wasn't exceptional. "There were thirty American kids at Kerem B'Yavneh, and maybe one or two stayed in Israel. So, I got to be a martyr, to say that I wanted to stay in Israel but my parents made me come home. The truth is, I used it mostly as an excuse."

Yeshiva University circa 1970 was a fortress of modern Orthodoxy, headquartered in a Moorish Revival building in the Upper Manhattan neighborhood of Washington Heights. Once home to German Jewish and Greek immigrants, the area was quickly becoming predominantly Hispanic, which made it feel foreign and forbidding to many of Yeshiva's not very streetwise or diversity-minded students. Yechiel never liked the neighborhood or the city in general. "I was constantly afraid of getting mugged or beaten up," he says. "I hated using the subways. It was scary to me just to be on the street."

The year Yechiel arrived, the university, to comply with federal regulations, decoupled its rabbinical school from the rest of the campus, but every undergraduate student still had to take a full course of Talmudic studies along with his major. The student body remained completely Jewish, campus dining was strictly kosher, and there was a no-girls-allowed policy. Women attended Stern College, YU's sister school, located safely downtown.

Yechiel roomed with Joe Telushkin, a graduate of the Flatbush Yeshiva. Telushkin was worldlier than his roomie, and more political, but they shared a love of speculation and spent a lot of time sitting around the dorm room on 186th Street ruminating on the meaning of life. Telushkin, who went on to become a rabbi and best-selling author, recalls Yechiel as "full of pure piety." He could also be a bit prissy. When Telushkin cursed or voiced an impious thought, Eckstein would admonish him with a rabbinical aphorism: "When you talk that way, you create a bad angel in the world." Telushkin was impressed that his roommate always got up for morning prayers, no matter how late they had been up the night before. He saw that Yechiel was moody, but he didn't recognize signs of clinical depression. "He had no idea how hard it was for me to get out of bed for any reason," Yechiel says. "I didn't want to but I knew I was supposed to. It was a matter of the discipline I had been taught. I was a yeshiva bocher, a rabbinical student, and that's what you were supposed to do."

Opposition to the war in Vietnam was igniting campuses around the country, but Yeshiva, inward-looking and politically conservative, was quiet. Most of the students were working toward rabbinical degrees and were exempt from the draft. Telushkin was an antiwar activist, but Yechiel's only protesting was done on behalf of the movement to free Soviet Jewry. He had no serious opinion about

Vietnam or other non-Jewish political issues, and very little free time for activism in any case. The need to support himself kept him busy with part-time jobs and trying to keep hunger pangs at bay.

His sister Ahuva had recently married Gary Epstein, a former editor of the Yeshiva University student newspaper who was struggling to make it as a writer. The young couple had a small apartment in a residential hotel, and Yechiel often came for dinner. Ahuva—who had suffered with Yechiel through their parents' stinginess with food—was happy to feed her growing brother and his insatiable appetite.

To supplement his income, Yechiel, who had been a song leader at Jewish summer camps, became a professional singer. He appeared on the religious entertainment circuit with groups like the Rabbis' Sons and Kol Salonika. He wore his hair long and occasionally donned a belt with a cowboy buckle, an extreme sartorial step in his world. Joe Telushkin recalls him as a "heartthrob." He dated, but always Orthodox girls, and he remained a "good boy," saving himself for marriage. Still, heartthrobs, kosher or not, weren't what the rabbis at Yeshiva University were interested in producing. The sterner faculty members considered even scrupulously chaste dating unacceptable, and public singing in mixed company unseemly and un-Jewish. "At our concerts there were lots of girls from Stern College, but we didn't mingle much," Eckstein says. "Nobody threw any hotel keys on the stage, that's for sure."

"Yechiel was underrated in the seminary because of his singing and his long hair," says Telushkin. "There were teachers who called him 'pretty boy,' which was not a compliment. They underestimated his intellect. When we sat around talking Torah, I was impressed by his insights. All these years later I still remember things he said about the meaning of freedom in Jewish tradition that made me see familiar things in a new way."

In addition to his rabbinical studies, Yechiel majored in psychology, but it didn't excite him. He began reading forbidden books by liberal Jewish thinkers and even Christian theologians. He was curious about Eastern religions, and the intellectual trends in secular America. This kind of curiosity and openness was frowned upon. "As a university, Yeshiva was third-rate," says Irving "Yitz" Greenberg, an Orthodox rabbi and Harvard PhD who served YU as a one-man American history department. "Yechiel was relatively liberal and he was bored by the second-rate secular scholarship and the doctrinaire theology of the faculty, mostly old men who barely spoke English and didn't have an appreciation for Western civilization. Some faculty members disliked him because he asked too many questions. But he wasn't rebelling, he was just looking for a more affirmative take on American life and the intersection between Judaism and other religions. A lot of older faculty disrespected Christianity and Christians. Yechiel didn't."

The interfaith issue—how Jews could and should relate to Christianity in the modern world—was a controversial one. In 1965, while Yechiel was in high school, the Second Vatican Council published *Nostra Aetate*, a rethinking of the church's attitude toward other religions, particularly Judaism. The document altered the traditional teaching that salvation is possible only through Roman Catholicism; it would now be available to "the whole people of God." For the first time in modern history, the Roman Catholic Church accepted the idea that God's biblical covenant with Israel also applied to present-day Jews. The church no longer claimed to be "the New Israel," a successor to the original chosen people. The notion that present-day Jews were accountable for the murder of God, and the anti-Semitism that naturally flowed from it, were renounced.

Jews debated how to react to these revolutionary changes. The political and community establishment, largely secular and liberal, was inclined to explore the opportunity for new religious coalitions. The Reform movement, soon to become the largest Jewish denomination, was glad to enter dialogue with the right kind of Christians—mainline Protestants as well as Catholics (no one contemplated any such connection with Christian fundamentalists). There were certain social taboos—in the mid-1960s even Reform rabbis frowned on intermarriage—but they were certainly in favor of friendship and cooperation.

The Conservative movement, always torn between Orthodoxy and Americanism, was ambivalent, but the scales were tipped by its most luminous thinker, Abraham Joshua Heschel, who taught at the denomination's flagship Jewish Theological Seminary. Heschel, the product of a distinguished Orthodox lineage, came to the United States from Europe in 1940, at the age of thirty-three. Though he was steeped in both Talmud and German philosophy, he Americanized rapidly, and gained fame marching with Martin Luther King Jr. in the South and involving himself in other American political issues. He was also active in the Vatican II process, lobbying for liberalization and insisting that Roman Catholicism accept Judaism as a religion with its own inherent spiritual value, not merely an unfulfilled early iteration of Christianity.

In 1965, Heschel delivered a speech at the Union Theological Seminary, perhaps the most prestigious mainline Protestant seminary in the country. His appearance there was, in itself, a remarkable development. In his remarks he made it clear that Judaism should no longer isolate itself from the modern world, and called for an alliance of Jews and Christians to fight against what he saw as their common foes: nihilism, desanctification of the Bible, and efforts to remove religion from the public square. Jews and Christians, he said, practiced different religions, but prayed to and were accountable before the same God.

Heschel's position was not welcomed by the Orthodox world and its most influential rabbis. Menachem Schneerson, a solitary, mystical figure, known as the Lubavitcher Rebbe, was dedicated to returning unbelieving Jews to the fold, not interacting with Christians. Reb Moshe Feinstein, the most influential Talmudic authority of his generation, denounced Vatican II as "a plague," spread by a pope "whose entire purpose is to cause the Jews to abandon their faith" by means of honeyed words.

Rabbi Joseph Soloveitchik, the head of Yeshiva University, was more ecumenical than Feinstein and Schneerson. A Talmud scholar of the first rank, he was also an intellectual, with a PhD in philosophy from the University of Berlin and—even more exceptional in the Orthodox world—a wife with a PhD of her own. He affirmed the existence of a shared Judeo-Christian cultural tradition and acknowledged the Roman Catholic Church as a legitimate "faith community" with which Jews could cooperate on civic issues. But he drew the line at interfaith dialogue that delved into theological or ritual matters. There would be no discussion with outsiders about the nature of God, his relationship with and requirements of the Jewish people, or the proper modes of Jewish worship.

As a high school student, Eckstein had been blissfully ignorant of this raging debate. He was too young, and too detached from the non-Jewish world, to bother paying attention. At YU, he was more concerned with his personal problems and his relations with some of his less friendly teachers. In class with Rabbi Soloveitchik—an aloof instructor, known for embarrassing unprepared students—Yechiel positioned himself behind a pillar, where he wouldn't be called on, and sometimes surreptitiously read books by the heretical Heschel, hidden inside his copy of the Talmud. He was taken by Heschel's spirituality, and his critique of Orthodoxy as an overly intellectualized and ritualized form in which, as he wrote, "faith is completely replaced by creed, worship by discipline, love by habit; when the crisis of today is ignored because of the splendor of the past; when faith becomes an heirloom rather than a living fountain; when religion speaks only in the name of authority rather than with the voice of compassion."

There were no Heschels at the Yeshiva University rabbinical seminary, but there were teachers who stood out for their humanity and warmth. First among them was Rabbi Nissan Alpert. A disciple of the forbidding Rabbi Moshe Feinstein, Alpert was in no way a theological liberal, but he appreciated Yechiel's questioning intellect and counseled him on coping with his personal demons. "I wasn't the best student. I was strange. But Rabbi Alpert looked for the good in me. He was so nonjudgmental, so understanding that he made me struggle to be worthy. And I loved the fact that he was so down-to-earth. Every day he would have a coffee and Danish across the street at a coffee shop, reading the *New York Times*, a secular newspaper. I could just go in and shoot the breeze with him, which was amazing. He was a black hat [ultra-Orthodox], of course, but he grew up in Brooklyn, he spoke good English, and he was a modern man." In the years when Eckstein was a pariah in Orthodox synagogues, he often took consolation in his relationship with Alpert. "I think that if he had lived to see what I've done with my life, he would have been very proud. He would have stuck up for me. I loved him and I miss him. I can never forget his last word—*'bitachon'* [a Hebrew term used to signify implacable faith]. That's how he lived and how he faced death." Eckstein was a young man when Alpert died, but he still refers to him—and no one else—as "my Rebbe."

In 1973, Yechiel graduated from YU with a bachelor's degree in psychology. He was happy to be out of school. "I felt that college had been something to do and get over with. That's all. Just a thing to get past." That summer he traveled to Jerusalem to appear in the Chassidic Song Festival, performing a new tune based on the saying of the eighteenth-century Hasidic rabbi, Nachman of Breslov: "All the world is a very narrow bridge / And the main thing is not to be afraid." The song was the hit of the festival and his recording of it was played often on Israeli radio.

He and a classmate rented an apartment in Jerusalem, where he spent the summer volunteering in a program aimed at helping newly arrived Russian immigrants to settle into the country. The roommates talked excitedly about the chance they might bring a girl back to the apartment and worked out a sign for ensuring privacy, a necktie hung on the doorknob of the bedroom.

It was just talk. The plan was never activated. Eckstein, still a romantic, was looking for the girl of his dreams, and he found her on the porch of the King David Hotel. He was coming out of the pool, where he swam a mile each day, when he saw her. Her eyes met his with what he interpreted as a welcoming glance, and he came over and introduced himself. Bonnie Siegman was nineteen years old, a rising sophomore at Barnard. She was a modern Orthodox girl from Long Island—her father, Henry Siegman, was an ordained rabbi—but she seemed to Yechiel to be a rare and exotic specimen of hip New Yorker. Bonnie was conversant in all manner of things he knew nothing about—Plato, Jane Austen, geology, the *New York Times*—and she was easy to talk to. He went back to his apartment and told his roommate that he had met the girl he was going to marry. Bonnie was almost perfect. Her only flaw, in Yechiel's eyes, was her height. "I've always been attracted to tall, graceful women. Bonnie was small and petite, and that made her not a perfect ten. My mother was a perfect ten, and I felt I deserved one."

For their first date, Yechiel picked Bonnie up at her grandparents' home in Tel Aviv. They were Holocaust survivors, members of the city's prosperous middle class, modern Orthodox establishment; Shlomo Goren, the Ashkenazi chief rabbi of Israel, was their neighbor. They fed Yechiel a home-cooked meal, asked a few questions— father a rabbi, check; plans to become one himself, double check—and pronounced him kosher.

After two weeks, Bonnie went back to New York, and Yechiel soon followed. She introduced him to the Manhattan cultural scene he had dimly perceived—museums, concerts, opera. One night she invited him to see *The Nutcracker*. It was his first ballet, but he spent the performance poring over notes with a flashlight, cramming for a test the next day in how to ritually slaughter a bull. Yechiel visited her at the Barnard dorm and was astonished to find that he was allowed to visit her in her room, unchaperoned. "Her roommate would leave and we were by ourselves," he recalls. "That was unheard-of!" Some of the guys at YU had bragged about going on "tefillin dates," taking along the phylacteries needed for morning prayers, but Yechiel was a virgin and would remain one until his wedding night. Still, the very idea of being alone with a beautiful young woman, on an Ivy League campus, in the heart of the sexual revolution, was intoxicating.

On October 6, 1973, the Egyptian and Syrian armies launched a surprise attack on Israel. It was Yom Kippur, the holiest day of the Jewish year, and Eckstein was in shul, in Canada. His first impulse was to get on a plane and volunteer. He had been too young for the Six-Day War. He had declined the paratroopers to go to Yeshiva

University. Now was his chance. "My mother told me that I shouldn't go—there was nothing I could do to help. Once again, it was Jackson to Eckstein, my parents dismissing my dreams." If he enlisted, he knew, he would be in the thick of the fighting. Moses's admonition to the cowardly tribes once again rang in his ears. How could he stand aside while his brothers fought? He didn't know how to fire a gun or drive a tank, but he could play the guitar and sing. A friend who worked for the Israeli Ministry of Education put him in touch with an officer in the Golani infantry brigade. If Yechiel could get himself to Israel, they would organize a tour for him, entertaining troops.

Eckstein's performances were one-man shows, just him and an acoustic guitar. His first show was for a hospital ward full of badly wounded soldiers. He walked in feeling self-conscious, but his mood lightened when one of the patients called out, "It's Tom Jones!" and everyone cracked up. He sang a set of Israeli songs, closing with his hit of the previous summer, "Narrow Bridge." When he finished, one of the soldiers told him he had been thinking of that song when he was guarding a bridge over the Suez Canal. Accompanied by an army jeep driver, Eckstein visited bases on the Syrian front. At one, he came under attack while he was singing. It was his baptism of fire.

Wandering around the front lines, Yechiel had felt the absence of a close friend and partner. He missed Bonnie, and when he returned to New York they resumed their relationship. Things went quickly; they were married the following September, less than a year after they met at the King David pool. They were both still in school, but in the Yeshiva University set this wasn't considered too young for matrimony.

The courtship had gone smoothly, although his first meeting with the Siegman family got off to a rocky start. Yechiel was invited to come out to West Hempstead, on Long Island, for a Shabbat meal. He was on his way when his train broke down. Afraid that it wouldn't get moving again before sundown, he explained his predicament to a fellow passenger, handed over his wallet and other items that Jews are forbidden to carry on the Sabbath, and asked the passenger to drop the stuff at Bonnie's house. Then he got off the train and began hiking. He arrived to his first meeting with his future in-laws sweaty and four hours late. When he explained the reason for the delay, Bonnie and her mother seemed relieved that nothing terrible had happened. But Yechiel detected a look of snide amusement on the face of Bonnie's father. "He didn't seem to be impressed by the fact that I didn't violate the Sabbath."

Henry Siegman was born in Belgium in 1930, immigrated to the United States, and served as a decorated Jewish chaplain in the Korean War. He was a rising star in the Jewish organizational world who went on to become the executive director of the American Jewish Congress, a Jewish advocacy group now all but extinct. The Siegman home was a testimony to Henry's prominence. The walls featured photos of him with the pope, foreign dignitaries, and American politicians. At the dinner table, Henry recounted his exploits and expounded on his ideas, dominating the conversation. If he was interested in his daughter's fiancé, it wasn't apparent. Still, Yechiel was impressed and intimidated by this formidable older man, and hurt that his future father-in-law seemed so distant. He saw that Bonnie hung on his every word and gazed at him with loving admiration. "When I mentioned later how her father snubbed me, Bonnie defended him as simply a man with European manners. I never believed that. He was just condescending and cold."

Sy and Belle were happy with Bonnie, although they, too, commented on how short she was compared with the Eckstein ideal. They liked Bonnie's mother, too, and considered her *heimish* (down-home) and easy to get along with. Henry was Henry, no more interested in them than he was in Yechiel or anyone else.

Bonnie and Yechiel were married in 1974, by Rabbi Alpert. On the surface they were a model modern Orthodox couple—attractive, wellborn, and committed, as their ancestors had been, to life within the boundaries and loyalties of Jewish life. Bonnie was finishing a degree in political science and working toward a teacher's certificate. By the time she was done, Yechiel would be a rabbi like his father before him, and bring honor to the Eckstein clan. No one would have taken him for a subversive.

But he was, at least a subversive in training. While at the Yeshiva he surreptitiously enrolled in a graduate program in religion at Columbia University, a program that was run jointly with the Union Theological Seminary. "I was graduating with an MA in Jewish philosophy from YU and feeling not smart—I was dating a Barnard girl, after all—as well as an alienation from the narrow way I had been raised. I wanted to escape the YU syndrome I had been in since high school. Most of all, I wanted to look at Judaism not just from a parochial Orthodox perspective but more objectively, from the outside in, the way that Heschel did."

Eckstein had applied to a graduate program at Fordham University, a Catholic school in the Bronx, and was rejected. "As a goof I applied to Columbia and they took me. I still don't know why, but they did. For me being able to say that I was studying at an Ivy League school was really exciting. It put me up to Bonnie's level, and it said to the world that I'm smart. I felt that the experience was something Bonnie and I could share. But she wasn't impressed. Whenever I mentioned in conversation that I was a student at Columbia, she made fun of me for being a name-dropper. Which, of course, I was."

Setting foot in a Christian school of theology like Union would probably have been grounds for expulsion by Yeshiva University. This was an act of intellectual rebellion, the first time in his life he had stepped out of the mold. He was thrilled by his own daring, but he also felt he was doing something wrong.

Kosher restaurants were hard to find near Columbia, so Eckstein ate lunch in the dining hall of the nearby Jewish Theological Seminary, the flagship institution of Conservative Judaism. He was studying Buddhism at Columbia, and Christianity at Union Theological, but in a way this culinary apostasy was worse; Orthodox Judaism regarded Conservatism as an especially threatening competitor. A few years earlier, Sy Eckstein's brother had been appointed rabbi of a Conservative synagogue in New York and the family was invited to his formal installation. Sy had consulted with Reb Moshe Feinstein himself about the propriety of attending the event.

Feinstein ruled that it was absolutely forbidden. "I felt like I was committing a sin every time I had lunch," Eckstein recalls.

At Columbia, Yechiel met David Ellenson, a Reform rabbinical student who was also working toward a PhD in religion. Ellenson was a Reform Jew, the first that Yechiel had ever encountered, and the two became friends. It helped that Ellenson had been raised in an Orthodox congregation; he was able to explain Reform practices—renunciation of the Talmud as source of binding law, mixed seating in synagogues, a lax attitude toward Sabbath observance and non-kosher food—in ways that made them seem less like laziness or assimilation than calculated variations on Jewish ritual and theological tradition. "David made me see and respect new things. It was exciting. Not only was I in the Ivy League, I was friends with a Reform rabbi."

For Yechiel, being at Columbia was a life-changing experience. For one thing, it was the first time he had attended a non-Jewish school. Things that couldn't be questioned were open to discussion there. It was especially startling to find himself on a campus where girls and guys intermingled. "At first I felt awkward—this wasn't how I was raised. But I loved the freedom. At YU you were expected to study Torah whenever you had free time. At Columbia, kids were just hanging out, just being." Ellenson recalls seeing Yechiel staring raptly at the quad and declaring it the most beautiful campus on earth. "He realized he was entering a bigger world," he says, "and he was very taken with it." On some level, it also made him nervous. He was jeopardizing his future and, for all he knew, his soul. But its attractions—and especially the opportunity to engage in unfettered intellectual exploration—trumped his concerns. Bonnie, who was used to the secular freedom of an Ivy League campus, encouraged him to expand his horizons.

After finishing his MA in Jewish philosophy at Yeshiva University, Eckstein began work on a doctoral thesis at Columbia. His subject was religious authority, and it involved a comparison of three leading Jewish thinkers—Joseph Soloveitchik, Abraham Heschel, and the Reform rabbi Eugene Borowitz—with the Protestant theologians Paul Tillich, Karl Barth, and Soren Kierkegaard. He was struck by similarities in the beliefs. The Reform notion that ultimate religious authority resides in the individual seemed similar to Kierkegaard's Christian existentialism. Heschel found authority in the collective experience of the Jewish people, rather than in holy texts; Tillich took a similar position regarding Christians. Barth's unease with liberal theology reminded Eckstein of Soloveitchik. Comparing and speculating, Eckstein found himself in the position of outside observer, a new and heady experience for a lifelong insider in Jewish Orthodoxy.

This way of thinking might have made for an interesting doctoral thesis, and Eckstein put a year and a half's worth of work into compiling research. But he never got a chance to write it up; instead, his academic career was cut short by a bizarre theft. In those pre-computer days, his research was all on three-by-five index cards, which he kept in his briefcase. Bonnie, student teaching at the time, parked their car next to a school and inadvertently left the door unlocked; the briefcase was stolen by what must have been a mystified and disappointed thief.

Eckstein had no copy, nor did he have the time or energy to reconstruct the work he had done. Not only that, it would have meant staying an extra semester and spending $500, money he didn't have, to retain his student status. In the end, Columbia gave him an M Phil, a master of philosophy, a degree that signifies completion of all but his dissertation. In 1984, he published a book, *What Christians Should Know about Jews and Judaism*, and petitioned Columbia to accept it in lieu of his thesis. The request was turned down on the grounds that the book was "fine for its intended audience," but "not appropriate as a piece of academic research." It was difficult to dispute that judgment, and Eckstein didn't.

In retrospect, the theft was a stroke of fortune. Had he finished the degree, he might have wound up in the wrong profession. "Yechiel is smart as hell," says Ellenson, who went on to a distinguished career as a professor and eventually as the president of Hebrew Union College. "But he didn't have an academic temperament."

He also had no money and no job. Worse, although he was now a rabbi, there were no full-time pulpits to be had. He had already been a weekend rabbi for a small shul in Jersey City, and it had been a miserable experience. He and Bonnie had to sleep on cots in the synagogue and eat their Shabbat meals, precooked and unheated, from paper plates. The synagogue was smelly and uncomfortable. Bonnie made it clear that she didn't like it, and after a few months she refused to continue. From then on Yechiel went by himself and struggled to get accustomed to spending his weekends alone.

Then opportunity came in an unexpected and unconventional

form. Yechiel was friendly with Rabbi Wolfe Kelman, a disciple of Heschel. As the head of the Conservative Rabbinical Assembly, Kelman knew of a congregation in Nashville looking for a rabbi. Yechiel, with his Canadian sincerity and easygoing manner, seemed like he might be a good fit. He flew down to Tennessee, spent a Shabbat at the synagogue, and was offered the job. It was tempting. The money—$25,000 a year to start—would go a long way in Tennessee. But Bonnie, a lifelong New Yorker, reacted to the idea of living in Nashville with the same reluctance that Yechiel's great-grandmother Gitel had shown toward Little Rock. It didn't seem like a good place to raise Jewish children.

Sy Eckstein, of course, was completely opposed to his son's defecting to the hated Conservatives, no matter which side of the Mason-Dixon Line they were found. Yechiel himself had reservations about leading a non-Orthodox synagogue. He liked the idea of pastoring to a community, preaching sermons and working with young people, but he knew from experience that rabbis were at the beck and call of everyone with a family event to perform, a personal problem to solve, or a complaint to make. He had seen firsthand how little power congregational rabbis have over financial matters; he never forgot his mother crying because the president of the shul in Ottawa wouldn't authorize the money for a new living room carpet.

Eckstein also knew that congregational rabbis had no privacy. "I'd be looking over my shoulder all the time, trying to make a good impression, not offending anyone. I didn't want to live a life where my religiosity was fueled by social fear or the need to maintain an image. I wanted religion to be genuine, to flow from within." Ultimately he turned down the job. He had listened to his heart—and to his wife—but he was still broke and unemployed.

It was Henry Siegman who came up with a solution. The Anti-Defamation League, the premier Jewish civil rights organization, was looking for a bright young man to take over Christian-Jewish relations. The national director in New York was slated to retire within two years, and Eckstein could then take over as ADL's national liaison with non-Jewish religious denominations and organizations. Until then, he could do the same in the Midwest. Bonnie was still hesitant to leave New York, but Chicago was certainly better than Tennessee.

In the clubby world of New York Jewish community organizations, it hardly mattered that Yechiel had two master's degrees, or an ordination signed by Rabbi Soloveitchik himself. "At that time, it was very rare for religious guys with yarmulkes to go to work for a secular Jewish organization," Eckstein recalls. Nate Perlmutter, the head of the ADL, was an ex-infantry officer, a plainspoken Brooklyn lawyer who once wrote a book on how to win at the racetrack. Perlmutter's assistant, Abe Foxman, had a similarly exotic biography. Ten years Eckstein's senior, he had been born in World War II–era Poland, and as an infant he was turned over to a Catholic nanny for safekeeping. She raised him as a Catholic until the end of the war, when his parents recovered him and brought him to Brooklyn. Foxman had studied at the prestigious Flatbush Yeshiva High School and City College, and got a law degree from New York University—and he was a talented and ambitious bureaucrat with his eyes on the eventual prize of leadership.

Eckstein wasn't convinced he fit in, or that he was the right guy for the ADL, but he took a risk and agreed to take the job. "Because my model for organizational leadership was Henry Siegman, I wasn't sure I could measure up," he says. "But I believed in interfaith work, even then, and if Nate Perlmutter thought I could do it, I was willing to give it a try. Fact is, I needed a job."

Four

❖

SWEET HOME CHICAGO

Eckstein was twenty-five years old when he and Bonnie first arrived in Chicago in 1976. His entire life had been spent inside a series of concentric Jewish circles—his father's synagogue, Jewish summer camps, Yeshiva High School, Israel, Yeshiva University, the religion program at Columbia University. Now he was being dispatched to a strange city to rally support from Christians, people with whom he had virtually no contact beyond the elite Protestant liberals he had met at Union Theological Seminary.

"I used to joke that the ADL decided to send me to the coldest place in the United States—that they sent me to Chicago because the Buffalo office was taken," he says. "But really, I liked Chicago. It had a civility I didn't find in New York, and once Bonnie and I moved into the Jewish neighborhood in Rogers Park, I felt a sense of community."

To Eckstein, Chicago was a temporary posting. He expected to go back to New York within two years, to the main office as the ADL's Christian liaison. At the time he arrived, interfaith issues were hot. Not long before, the American Nazi Party had announced plans to march through Skokie, a suburb with a large Jewish population and many Holocaust survivors. The American Civil Liberties Union, whose leadership was largely Jewish, supported the march, on First Amendment grounds. The ADL and other Jewish organizations strongly opposed it, and the split caused tension. Eckstein was torn. "My personal feeling at the time was that it was a mistake to oppose the Nazi marches. Better to ignore it than to give them free publicity. But I certainly understood the position of the Holocaust survivors who said that Hitler started out small too. In any case, I was part of the ADL and we had to represent the community and its fears."

The events in Skokie were an illuminating moment in the changes that were taking place in Jewish-Christian relations in Chicago. For years, the city's liberal white Protestants had participated in brotherhood meetings with its liberal Jews. They marched together against the Vietnam War, increasingly shared the same zip codes, attended the same schools, and starting in the sixties, married one another. But liberal denominations were also moving in the direction of liberation theology, a doctrine which held that Christianity's essence was social justice—solidarity with people of color who had suffered under white colonialism. Activists in these mainline churches, who saw Palestinians as the legitimate native population of the Holy Land, began placing Israel on the side of the oppressors. This tendency got a public face in Illinois. Until 1982, Eckstein's district was represented in Congress by Paul Findley, perhaps the most openly anti-Israel representative in the history of the House. And in 1975, Senator Chuck Percy, a onetime Republican presidential hopeful, traveled to the Middle East, met with Yasser Arafat (still considered persona non grata by the US government), and called for Israel to return to its 1967 borders. The ADL and its allies were enraged.

The Chicago area is also home to the largest Polish Catholic community outside Warsaw, and to a very large community of German Catholics. Vatican II had helped to mitigate some of their traditional theological animosity toward Jews, but the history of virulent German and Polish anti-Semitism was always present, and became more acute in 1978 after NBC aired a popular miniseries about the Holocaust.

While all this was going on, the alliance between Jews and black Baptists, built during the civil rights era, had been badly frayed by political rivalry; the ascendant black minister and activist Jesse Jackson, a disciple of Martin Luther King Jr., did not share his mentor's instinctive Zionism or his Jewish political alliances. The openly anti-Semitic Black Muslims also had their national headquarters in the city.

Whatever issues the Jews of Chicago had with the contemporary civil rights establishment, or with mainline Protestant churches and the Roman Catholic Church, these groups were at least intelligible. Evangelicals were not. If there were no significant problems with Christian evangelicals, it was for the simple reason that Jews had no contact with them. To the Jewish organizational world, they were probable anti-Semites—American Cossacks to be watched with a sharp eye. They certainly weren't potential allies. When the Anti-Defamation League sent Eckstein to Chicago to foster interfaith relations, these were not the people it had in mind. A worldlier young man would have intuited this. He would have understood the mental map of America hanging in the ADL's war room—the kind of "good Gentiles" with whom it wanted to make common cause. But in the Orthodox circles in which Eckstein had been raised, all Christians were more or less just Christians.

Eckstein dutifully took up the challenges of his job. He taught a course, Understanding the Jews, for the Roman Catholic archdiocesan board of education. He addressed a conference of priests and nuns on how Jews and Christians speak to God. He organized a dialogue between Methodist ministers and a group of Chicago rabbis. He took part in brotherhood lunches, joint Holocaust memorials, and the other bland ecumenical ceremonies that were part of the life of any American Jewish interfaith bureaucrat.

The ADL was also a defense organization. Its New York leaders referred to it among themselves as "the Agency," as though it was a sort of Jewish CIA. National issues that took place in Chicago—such as Nazi marches or the anti-Jewish fulminations of the Chicago-based Jesse Jackson and Louis Farrakhan—were handled by the New York office. At first, Eckstein didn't bridle at this. He was satisfied to deal with the small irritants of Jewish life in the Midwest: Jews for Jesus missionizing in the suburbs, an elementary school putting on a Christmas pageant with "strong Christological emphasis," the Chicago Board of Education offering a curriculum on Genocide Through the Ages that never dealt specifically with the Holocaust. He handled the jobs energetically and tactfully, and got some credit for it. The *Chicago Sun-Times* named him one of its "79 People to Watch in '79." The following year, *People* included him in a list of up-and-coming young men and women. He started getting invited to training sessions for future Jewish leaders in New York, and it became clear that he was heading for a larger role in the organizational life of American Jewry.

In retrospect, it seems obvious that Yechiel Eckstein and the evangelical Christian community were made for one another. But at the time, the Pentecostal and Southern Baptist churches were just more Christian doors he was knocking on in his efforts to find allies. In mainline churches, he got a polite but often distant response. The evangelicals were different. At Baptist and Pentecostal churches, Eckstein found himself embraced as a long-awaited brother, a representative of God's chosen people. "I wasn't the first rabbi to meet with the cardinal or the big ministers," says Eckstein. "But I was the first Jew most of the evangelical pastors had ever met."

Very few American Jews regard themselves as "chosen people" in the literal sense. God talk tends to make even liberal rabbis uncomfortable. Orthodox Jews do believe in God and the concept of being a holy people, but they are not inclined to seek validation from Christians of any denomination or variety. Eckstein was raised to feel this way too. Yet he couldn't help noticing how responsive the evangelicals seemed, how eager they were to help him do his job by supporting Israel, Soviet Jewry, and other Jewish issues. Considering his mission, reaching out to them seemed like a practical thing to do. But there was more to it than simple pragmatism. Eckstein, to his surprise, found himself moved by their sincerity, their religious passion, and their unconditional love for God, Israel, and the Jewish people. And he was also cognizant that they represented an opportunity for bridge building.

Evangelical interest in the Jewish people was not restricted to Chicago. It was part of a national revival of fundamentalist political involvement. At the start of the twentieth century, evangelicals had real political power, but their greatest success—the enactment of Prohibition—turned into a national fiasco. The effort to ban the teaching of Darwinism in high schools resulted in mockery by big-city intellectuals, led by the biting polemicist H. L. Mencken. By the early 1930s, the political area didn't seem like a welcoming place, and evangelicals retreated into their churches, where nobody would laugh at them for believing in Adam and Eve, or curse them for cutting off their drinks. This retreat ended only in the late 1960s, when evangelicals saw American culture going from "one nation under God" to "sex, drugs, and rock 'n' roll." Boys with long hair marched in the streets declaring they wouldn't fight for their country. Half-naked girls derided marriage and talked openly about their right to birth control and abortion. Most evangelicals didn't listen to Bob Dylan (at least before his Christian period) but they instinctively felt the truth of his song "The Times They Are a-Changin'"—America's sons and daughters were truly beyond their parents' command.

In retrospect, it is obvious that a cultural shift of this magnitude would engender a counterrevolution. Politically it came in the Nixon landslide of 1972. Evangelicals, traditionally Democrats, began moving to the Republican Party and using politics as a vehicle for their social and religious conservatism. The leaders of this movement included two formidable preachers from Virginia, Jerry Falwell and Pat Robertson. They were at once contemporaries, allies, and rivals. Falwell came from a family of Lynchburg roughnecks; his father and uncles were, not to put too fine a point on it, gangsters, very far from Christian faith of any kind. Robertson was a Virginia aristocrat, a descendant of signers of the Declaration of Independence, whose father, Willis Robertson, represented their state in the US Senate. Each was a master of televangelism, raising huge sums for projects that included the founding of two Christian schools, Robertson's stately Regent University in Virginia Beach and Falwell's more populist Liberty University in Lynchburg. Both were dedicated to wresting the culture back from what they saw as the atheists, libertines, and socialists who had snatched control. And they shared one more essential belief: The creation of a Jewish state in Israel (and its defense by the United States) was a sign of God acting in history and fulfilling biblical prophecy.

In 1979, Falwell established the Moral Majority, a coalition of evangelical Christians whose founding document endorsed four fundamental positions: pro-life, pro–traditional family, pro–national defense—and pro-Israel. That same year, Robertson started the Christian Broadcasting Network and became host of *The 700 Club*, a talk show that made him the most widely heard evangelical voice

in the land. Robertson often spoke of the birth of Israel as a fulfillment of biblical prophecy.

Eckstein arrived in Chicago at a pivotal moment in relations between
the governments of Israel and the United States. In May of 1977, Menachem Begin was elected to lead a new ruling coalition. Unlike his
Labor Party predecessors, Begin was a deeply religious Jew. On election night, at the televised victory celebration, his first public act as
prime minister was to don a black yarmulke and recite psalms. It sent
an unmistakable message: The era of Israel's socialist, atheistic founders was over. To make it even clearer, he declared that the lands on the
West Bank of the Jordan River, which he called by their biblical names,
Judea and Samaria, were an inseparable part of the Jewish patrimony.

Three months after his election, Begin traveled to Washington
to meet the recently elected Jimmy Carter. Since the Six-Day War,
America's policy had been that Israel must withdraw from the territories in return for peace and secure borders. Israel had refused,
consciously echoing the Arab League's famous post–Six-Day War
dictum: "No negotiations, no recognition, and no peace." Under the
circumstances, American governments under Johnson, Nixon, and
Ford had been content to kick the can down the road.

Begin wanted more. He had hopes that President Jimmy Carter
might actually reverse American policy and agree that the territories
were not occupied but liberated. Carter, he reasoned, was a religious
man, a Baptist Sunday school teacher who knew the Bible. He came
to Washington to offer the American president a chance to go down

in history as the champion of God's plan for the unity of the Jewish homeland.

Carter didn't see it that way. The Bible was fine for sermons, but foreign policy was a different matter. America had interests in the Middle East—bolstering anti-Communist regimes, protecting oil supplies, and improving relations with restive Arab countries whose populations and UN votes dwarfed Israel's. Beyond that, Carter's Christianity leaned to liberation theology. The Jews had once been oppressed, sure, but they had achieved self-determination and sovereignty. Now it was the Palestinians' turn.

Never before had there been such a sharp and public disagreement between a Democratic president and an Israeli prime minister on such a fundamental issue. By and large, the American Jewish establishment sided with Carter. Most Jewish leaders were liberal secularists, comfortable arguing Israel's case on security grounds but less comfortable arguing that God had literally promised any real estate to the Jews— and they told Begin so. Undeterred, he went back to Israel and ordered an aggressive program of Jewish settlement in the disputed territories, which Carter condemned as illegal. The Jewish establishment, composed almost entirely of Democrats, didn't want to get crosswise with the administration. It pressed Begin to be flexible on the question of Jewish sovereignty in the territories, a demand Begin considered absurd.

Eckstein was in Chicago, watching these developments with growing concern. Among mainline Christians he often encountered Carteresque criticism of Israel's settlement policies and increasing sympathy for the Palestinians. Jews were worried that Israel was giving them a bad name. In private, many conceded that Carter was too harsh on Begin, but they were also concerned that standing up for Israel could raise questions about their loyalty to the United States. Eckstein himself was torn. He managed to spend his college years in New York without involving himself in the generational disputes over the Vietnam War, Watergate, or the other hot-button issues of the day. He was a registered Democrat simply because most Jews he knew were Democrats. Israel was his only real political concern, and he was temperamentally inclined to see both sides of the internal Jewish debate. It was clear to him that the entire Land of Israel, including Judea and Samaria, was promised by God to the people of Israel. But he wasn't necessarily convinced that this was the moment to collect. He knew that many patriotic Israelis didn't agree with the policy of the Begin government, and he could see the dangers posed by a growing Arab minority within the borders Israel controlled. At the same time, he also knew that Israel was in a precarious security and geopolitical situation and that many adherents of liberation theology, who objected on principle to a Jewish state in the Holy Land, were taking advantage of the settlement issue as a cloak for anti-Jewish resentments.

In his rounds, the only place Eckstein didn't encounter such doubts was among evangelical Christians. On the contrary: "These folks would sometimes get angry when they heard Israelis or Jews talking about 'giving back land to the Palestinians,'" he says. "Ministers would say to me, 'The land was given to the Jews by God; they don't have the right to give it away.'" Nor were evangelicals cowed in any way by the insinuations about the power of the Israeli lobby over American foreign affairs or accusations of dual loyalty. They quoted God's promise to Abraham and his progeny from Genesis 12:3: "I will bless those who bless you, and those who curse you I will curse." What could be simpler than that? These Baptists and Pentecostals were not concerned with the national rights of Palestinians—God had made no territorial promises to them. If the Arabs wanted self-determination, they had two dozen countries to choose from. And they were unimpressed by dire demographic predictions; if God wanted a Jewish majority, he would provide one (a belief that gained strength a decade later when a million Jews were unexpectedly released from the former Soviet Union and allowed to move to Israel). Here was a group constituting tens of millions of Americans that offered support and demanded nothing in return.

Like everyone else in the Jewish world, Eckstein was familiar with university studies claiming a connection between Christian fundamentalism and political extremism, even fascism. He had seen Hollywood portrayals of Pentecostals as ignorant southern bigots. At Union Theological Seminary, he had heard Christian liberals deride evangelicals as Neanderthal "fundies." But in Chicago he met evangelicals who didn't fit the mold. One was Morris Inch, the head of the Wheaton College biblical studies department. Inch was from Boston, spoke with a JFK accent, and exhibited a keen curiosity about how Jews understood the Bible. Through him, Eckstein met

Ed Hakes, the dean of Trinity College and, unexpectedly, a New Yorker. The three of them decided to hold a conference of Jews and Christians to explore possible areas of agreement and cooperation.

The conference took place at Trinity, in Deerfield, Illinois, early in 1979. Originally the plan had been to hold the meetings at Wheaton, the alma mater of Billy Graham, but some at the school were concerned that there would be a negative reaction to such an ecumenical gathering. At Wheaton's insistence, the conference was closed to the public and the press. On the Jewish side, the event took place under the auspices of the ADL, and included Jewish academicians and rabbis from all the denominations.

At the opening session, Dr. Inch surveyed the divide they were hoping to bridge. "As evangelicals we are willing to die for the Jews, but we still hardly know them," he said. David Wells, a noted evangelical scholar, drew a distinction between the traditionally hostile and sometimes violent anti-Jewish stance of Catholics and liberal Protestants and the philo-Semitism of the evangelicals. "We have a history of tolerance," he said. "We love Jews." At which point a rabbi rose and said, "If you really love us, you would leave us and our kids alone." He pointed out that Catholics and mainline Protestants no longer missioned among Jews, and demanded that the evangelicals follow their example.

Wells responded simply, "Rabbi, we can't do that."

Eckstein realized that this was the crux of the matter. Evangelicals are bound by what they call the Great Commission, the obligation to share their faith and lead nonbelievers, including Jews (and, historically, often Jews especially) to accept Jesus as their savior. For

Jews, the refusal to accept other religions has been axiomatic—the brightest of bright lines separating their community from those of non-Jews. After the Holocaust, this idea took on special gravity; as the theologian Emil Fackenheim put it, the Eleventh Commandment is Jewish survival.

To connect Jews and evangelicals would require more than simply holding meetings and professions of fellowship or of mutual support for the State of Israel. Eckstein needed to reconcile two contradictory obligations. It was clear that a genuine religious dialogue would not emerge if either side expected the other to sacrifice its core principle. He put himself in evangelical shoes, searching for a theological synthesis. He didn't find it that day, but over time he arrived at a formula, based on a distinction he drew between "witnessing" and "proselytizing."

Witnessing meant, in his terms, Christians sharing their faith and serving as an example of that faith in their daily lives. America is a country based on freedom of speech, after all. Everyone has the right to share his or her beliefs. The question is: How do you do it? And where does sharing cross the line? Eckstein set that line at deception, coercion, or specifically targeting Jews for conversion, and set out to convince evangelicals that they shouldn't cross it. But, he believed, if they were prepared to respect limits, they were natural and desirable allies.

"Until I came up with the synthesis principle, evangelicals (and other Christians) related to Jews through missionary activity. They had no other avenue. The novelty of what I did was to give Christians a tangible, meaningful, and orthodox way to deal with Jews without trying to convert them. They could make that contact by supporting Israel and the Jewish people. They had a positive alternative, something that wouldn't offend or threaten Jews. Christian missionary groups who target Jews hated me for that. It set back their activities. I hurt their business."

When the leaders of the ADL read Eckstein's reports, they thought that he had gone crazy in the wilds of the Midwest. To big-city apparatchiks, he came off as boyishly naive, lacking the knowing cynicism that sets the tone of sophisticated Jewish discourse in America. The "pure piety" he had displayed in the seminary, his fervent style of prayer and talk about his own personal relationship with God, seemed undignified, perhaps even a little bit "Christian." No one in the ADL's home office could imagine that these so-called Christian Zionists Eckstein was befriending were anything but trouble: crazed end-of-the-worlders who wanted to gather all the Jews in the Holy Land to speed up the final battle at Armageddon, missionaries out to capture Jewish souls, or simply bigots. There were domestic concerns as well; the secular Jewish community was concerned that rising evangelical political power would be detrimental to its values, imposing prayer in public schools, fighting the Supreme Court decision on a woman's right to an abortion, and generally bringing Christianity into the public square.

In August 1980, the Reverend Bailey Smith, president of the Southern Baptist Convention—America's largest Protestant denomination—gave a speech dismissing the value of Jewish prayer. "It is interesting," he said, "that at great political rallies . . . you have a Protestant to pray and a Catholic to pray, and then you have a Jew to pray. With all due respect to those dear people, my friend, God Almighty does not hear the prayer of a Jew. For how in the world can God hear the prayer of a man who says that Jesus Christ is not the true Messiah? It is blasphemy."

The speech got national attention, and it seemed to confirm the worst fears of the New York establishment. The ADL demanded a retraction. But Eckstein saw an opportunity. Reverend Smith may have been the head of a national denomination, but he was also a small-town preacher from Del City, Oklahoma, who had been shocked by the reaction to what, it seemed to him, was just common sense. If salvation could come only through Jesus, then the Jews who rejected him weren't going to be saved. He never gave a thought to how that might sound to the Jews themselves. It was a teachable moment. With Eckstein's encouragement, the ADL invited Smith to go on an educational mission to Israel, and he accepted, inviting a delegation of fellow Southern Baptist ministers to come with him. Eckstein led the group, along with an ADL representative from Dallas.

The delegation was warmly received by Prime Minister Begin, and was widely reported in the Israeli and international media. Begin was as religious in his way as his guests, but he was also a highly pragmatic politician who, having lost eight straight national elections before finally winning office, had few illusions about the efficacy of Jewish prayer. These ministers of the gospel shared his belief that the territories of Judea and Samaria were part of the Jewish patrimony. They would defend Israel from its American critics, and that was good enough for him. Begin ordered the red carpet rolled out.

One essential stop on the Israeli VIP tour was Yad Vashem, the Holocaust museum and memorial in Jerusalem. It was there that the bridge-building trip almost imploded. The Baptist ministers were, of course, aware that they had come to Israel in large part to pay penance for the remarks of Reverend Smith, but the need to proclaim over and over their goodwill toward the Jews and Israel grated on many. The implicit message of Yad Vashem—this is where the anti-Semitism of Christendom leads—was not at all well received. Yechiel, as group leader, added to the tension by referring to Hitler and the Nazis as Christians. He was interrupted by Pastor Ed Young Sr. "What do Christians have to do with this?" he demanded. "Hitler wasn't a Christian!"

Yechiel was taken aback. "It may be that the Holocaust wasn't carried out by devout Christians," he said mildly, "but the long history of Christian anti-Semitism certainly prepared the ground, wouldn't you agree?" Pastor Young emphatically did not. "Those people you are talking about who persecuted the Jews weren't Christians," he said. "They were *Catholics*. If they had been Christians, they would never have done such a thing!" The other pastors nodded in agreement.

To Eckstein, who was still not fully acquainted with evangelical parlance, this seemed a distinction without a difference. Catholics weren't Christians? Catholics and Baptists alike accepted the divinity of Jesus and the holiness of the New Testament. "I thought they were running away from the Christian history of anti-Semitism."

For centuries, Christian leaders and thinkers grappled with the paradox that God's chosen people were also those who had denied the

Son of God and even killed him. It was, for many, clear that the Jews, by refusing to accept Jesus as Messiah, were no longer God's elect; they had been replaced by the community of Christian believers. Saint Augustine himself established the doctrine, influential in Christendom for a thousand years, that Jews should be despised but tolerated as an object lesson in how God punishes those who disobey him.

The Crusaders slaughtered Jews under the banner of the cross. The priests of the Inquisition forced them to flee or accept Christ. In European lands where Jews were allowed to live, they were second-class citizens or worse, actual slaves of the emperor. Early in the sixteenth century, Martin Luther, a German Catholic priest, broke from his church and launched what came to be known as the Protestant Reformation. At first, Luther was a critic of anti-Semitism, accusing the Roman Catholic hierarchy of treating the Jews "like dogs rather than human beings" and reminding Christians that Jesus himself had been a Jew. "We must receive them cordially, and permit them to trade and work with us, that they may have occasion and opportunity to associate with us, hear our Christian teaching, and witness our Christian life," he wrote. "If some of them should prove stiff-necked, what of it? After all, we ourselves are not all good Christians either." It didn't take long for Luther to change his mind. In the face of Jewish resistance to his message, he denounced Christ's relatives as "a whoring people" whose "boast of lineage, circumcision and law must be accounted as filth." Luther called on his followers to burn down the Jews' homes and synagogues, seize their property, ban their books, and execute their rabbis.

These thoughts ran through Eckstein's mind, but he held his tongue. He believed that this mission to Israel was a key part of God's plan (and his) to bring about evangelical-Jewish reconciliation. Now it was in danger of blowing up in full view of the Israeli and world media—at Yad Vashem, no less. That night, at dinner with the ministers, he raised the issue again, as earnestly as he could: What did they mean when they said that Catholics aren't Christians?

The ministers explained that Catholics haven't directly and personally found salvation by surrendering to Jesus Christ and being baptized in the Holy Spirit. Catholics, they said, had a church hierarchy instead of an unmediated relationship with Jesus. "The pope may call himself a Christian, but he isn't born-again," one said.

Eckstein was surprised. If Jew hatred was a Catholic sin, how did the ministers explain Luther, Calvin, and the other Protestant anti-Semites? Surely they were Christians? Pastor Young disagreed. No true Christian, he said, could possibly hate the Jews, the apple of God's eye. In fact, the hatred of Jews itself demonstrated that anti-Semites aren't true Christians and never had been. Through the centuries, he explained, there had been a quiet, persistent "underground church" that was the true form of Christianity. These Christians had themselves been persecuted, not only by the Roman Catholic Church but by more doctrinaire Protestants. They were philo-Semites, like the Pilgrims who founded America. They venerated the Old Testament, had been embodied during the Holocaust by true Christians like Pastor Dietrich Bonhoeffer, and now longed for communion with the Jewish people.

This seemed to Eckstein to be a novel and self-serving history of Christian anti-Semitism. At the same time, it gave him pause. He was willing to look at the other side, grant it good faith, and try to see its perspective. If he wanted to be accepted as a Jew on his own terms, he was willing to grant these ministers their own self-understanding. The Catholic-Christian distinction was also a lesson in the nuances of evangelical English.

The crisis passed, the trip went on, and the travelers came to understand one another's sensitivities. One night in Haifa, Pastor Smith marveled over a local sweet. His host informed him that it was a rum ball. The minister stopped chewing and spit it into his napkin. "Oh my gosh," he said. "We don't touch alcohol. I hope nobody saw me." Yechiel thought it was strange until he put himself in the minister's place. "What if I had been eating from a salad bar and found out it had shrimp in it? I would have spit it out the same way."

At a party at the Sea of Galilee, the band broke into a hora, and people got up to do the traditional Jewish circle dance. Several of the pastors remained seated. When Yechiel tried to coax one of them onto the floor, he said, "All I need is for my congregation to see a picture of me dancing . . . with a rabbi, no less!"

The trip ended in success. Pastor Smith was grateful to Yechiel for helping him fend off charges of anti-Semitism. He invited the young rabbi to visit his congregation, where Eckstein preached on the subject of Jewish-evangelical fellowship. "It was my first time in a megachurch, with five thousand people present. There were a lot of reporters there, looking for another gaffe. I didn't really know what

Bailey was going to say, and he didn't know what I would say. We both walked on eggshells. When I was finished, a clearly relieved Reverend Smith embraced me and said, 'Isn't this rabbi terrific? We have to have him back for one of our crusades.' The congregation applauded. I didn't know how to respond, but I had to say something. So I said, 'Well, I'll be happy to come back, but maybe not for a crusade. That didn't work out too well for us the first time.'" The audience laughed and applauded. So did Smith. "From that time on, I had an open door to Southern Baptist congregations across the country," Eckstein says.

Every ten years, the president of the United States convenes an official commission on the Bible. In 1983, Eckstein was appointed the Jewish representative. Bill Bright, the founder of the Campus Crusade for Christ, was also a member. In a joint appearance, Bright strongly advocated bringing people to salvation through the Bible. Eckstein interrupted, "Which Bible?"

"The complete Bible, of course," said Bright, missing Eckstein's point—what they shared was the Old Testament.

Here was a chance for Eckstein to publicly unveil the synthesis he had been developing. "If I understand your theology," he said, "your Great Commission is not to convert people to Christ. It is to introduce them to the love of God through Christ. But it is God through the Holy Spirit who either does or does not bring about the conversion. And if God is sovereign, he can be trusted. He will do whatever he does in his own time, right?"

Bright conceded the point. That concession became an important milestone in the ability of evangelical leaders to rationalize their commitment to the Great Commission without antagonizing American Jews.

Around the same time, Eckstein participated in a televised debate on Paul Crouch's TBN show, *Praise the Lord*, with Hal Lindsey, author of *The Late Great Planet Earth*, a best seller about the book of Revelation and its view of end times. Lindsey argued that the mass killings of the Rapture would make the Holocaust "look like a tea party." Eckstein took offense at the juxtaposition, but he used the occasion for further bridge building. "We Jews, over centuries, have rejected predictions," he said. Indeed, the Talmud notes that when the Second Temple was destroyed, the gift of prophecy was given to fools, although Eckstein diplomatically left that unsaid. He pointed out that the Jewish attitude toward prophecy is to look back in history and identify its operation. "The establishment of Israel, for example, may well be a fulfillment of divine prophecy. Time will tell. But acting on unfulfilled promises of the Bible can be dangerous."

On this subject, Eckstein had an evangelical amen corner. Christian Zionists like Robertson and Falwell believed there would come a final battle between Satan and God, at Armageddon, in which people who have accepted Jesus as their savior will be raptured up to heaven. *But*—they saw this as God's work, done in God's time. As Falwell told Eckstein in a meeting at Liberty University, it is an act of arrogance for humans to try to speed up or change God's plans. What is incumbent on Christians is to follow the biblical commandment to bless Israel with support.

———

In 1983, the ADL asked Eckstein to return to the main office in New York and take on national interfaith activities. He was wary. New York meant engaging in office politics and accepting the authority of people with whom he fundamentally disagreed on this question of Jewish-evangelical relations. He said he would come to the home office on condition that he report directly to Nate Perlmutter. It would have moved him up in the organization in a way that was bound to elicit opposition, and it did. When the ADL called his bluff, he left.

Yechiel and Bonnie, together with their first two daughters, Tamar and Talia, decided to remain in Chicago. The family had a modest house in Skokie, and Eckstein had become prominent in the city. "Reporters noticed Yechiel," says Bruce Buursma, the religion writer for the *Chicago Tribune* at the time. "I knew a lot of rabbis in those days, but he stood out. For one thing, he looked more like a Big Ten quarterback than a clergyman. He was very extroverted and open, a lover of people and experiences, not at all parochial, if you can say that about a rabbi. And he had a tendency to listen more than he talked, which is a pretty unusual trait in just about anybody." For years, Eckstein had cultivated and befriended reporters like Buursma on behalf of the ADL. Now he was ready to advocate for his vision. To do all this, he needed an organization. And so he founded one, a one-man show he grandly named the Holyland Fellowship of Christians and Jews.

Five

❖

FELLOWSHIP

In 1982, Mary Fleming—twenty-two years old, a nice Catholic girl from the suburbs—arrived at the ADL as a temporary secretary. She didn't know a thing about Judaism, much less the activities of the Anti-Defamation League. She had never met a rabbi before. Her initial assignment was to type a manuscript Eckstein had written in longhand, *What Christians Should Know about Jews and Judaism*. She recalls, "Working on the manuscript was like a personal introductory course."

Yechiel was thirty-one and seemed old to Mary, but she was struck by his informal style. "There was nothing holier than thou about him," she recalls. "We talked about the boys I was dating and he gave me advice when I asked for it." In fact, she was far worldlier than her boss. One night Yechiel agreed to join her and her boyfriend for a drink at their favorite South Side Irish bar. "It was kind of a rough place—scantily dressed women and guys who got a little rowdy. I remember how Yechiel took it all in. He seemed amazed, like he was seeing something he had never even imagined. It tickled him, I think."

When Yechiel left the ADL, Mary went with him. Together they opened up a two-room office in the Carson Pirie Scott building on South Wabash, in downtown Chicago. An elevated train ran right outside their window, which never closed properly. The place was furnished with used furniture and metal filing cabinets. Yechiel didn't have enough money to hire her full-time; she worked four or five evenings a week, from five thirty to nine thirty. Yechiel was always there when she arrived, and he was still there when she left.

Eckstein was always broke. To pay the bills he took all sorts of part-time gigs, the most lucrative of which was forming an orchestra of Jewish music in partnership with a Chicago bandleader named Don Cagen. Eckstein loved to sing, and his songs were always strictly kosher (no sexy crooning allowed!), but it sometimes bothered him that he was making his living that way. "I was a rabbi, and here I was a wedding singer. I could get people out of their seats and onto the dance floor—but I felt it wasn't dignified. I did it for the money. I was making between $1,000 and $1,300 a night, about $20,000 a year, which was very good money back then."

On Shabbat, Yechiel worked as a part-time rabbi for a downtown congregation that met in the Park Hotel. Since he couldn't travel back and forth from Skokie on the Sabbath, Bonnie and the girls spent their weekends there. "It was Jersey City all over again," he recalls. He delivered sermons, led prayers, and fulfilled pastoral duties for the synagogue. On Sundays he went from one evangelical church to another in the Chicago area. He'd come back to work on Monday with a list of people who expressed interest in what he began calling his ministry. He sent each one a personal letter asking for a contribution, and recorded their replies on three-by-five index cards. Every two weeks, the Fellowship deposited the fruits of Eckstein's labors in a Chicago branch of Bank Leumi, one of Israel's biggest banks. Money came in slowly; some days Yechiel waited by the mailbox, hoping for a check that would allow him to cover the rent or pay the electric bill. That first year, the income of the Fellowship was $26,679. Eckstein's salary was $9,400.

It was, perforce, a very tight ship. Eckstein monitored every expenditure, down to the cost of paper clips. When he did bulk mailings, he took them to the post office himself to save the expense of a delivery service. He made a daily list of items that required his attention and when he finished an item, he erased it in order to save paper. Although he and Mary were on friendly terms, she found him a demanding boss. "He checked everything, and no detail was too small to escape his notice," she recalls. "He'd look for mistakes and correct them himself. He was never harsh, but he made it clear that everything had to be perfect."

When he wasn't busy with rabbinical duties, trying to find supporters in the pews of evangelical churches, or stealing time with his young daughters, Eckstein made the rounds of the wealthy Jews of Chicago looking for financial support. Many of them had followed his career at the ADL and considered him a bright young man with rather eccentric ideas. Among them was Bob Asher, a wealthy businessman and former president of the American Israel Public Affairs Committee (AIPAC). Yechiel set forth his vision of millions of Christian Zionists supporting Israel because of their belief in the Bible. Asher, who like most of the other Jewish community leaders was not especially pious, was respectful but dubious. He gave Yechiel a small donation and, more importantly, wrote letters of introduction to other pro-Israel philanthropists around the country. Most of them didn't want anything to do with evangelicals. Some reacted with anger. But a few gave enough money to keep the Fellowship afloat. Among the early donors were Max Fisher of Detroit, one of the country's leading Republican moneymen; the owner of the Chicago White Sox, Bob Mazer, who went on to become chairman of the Fellowship's board of directors; and the Massachusetts businessman Robert Lappin (who later gained national fame by replenishing his employees' retirement funds after he invested them with the Ponzi scammer Bernie Madoff). Even if none of them were convinced that Eckstein's vision would become reality, they thought it was worth a small gesture to encourage him.

Most of Eckstein's Jewish donors were Republicans. But he also found an improbable—and reluctant—supporter in Chicago's Philip Klutznick, a multimillionaire real estate developer and investor and former president of the World Jewish Congress. Klutznick was a lifelong Democrat who served in various roles during the Kennedy and Johnson administrations and as secretary of commerce under Jimmy Carter. Shortly after Eckstein founded the Fellowship, Klutznick came to the Ritz Hotel for a chat, and the two began corresponding. In September 1984, just before Jerry Falwell and Pat Robertson came to Chicago to participate in Eckstein's first Day of Christian and Jewish Solidarity with Israel, Klutznick, who was forty years older than Eckstein, wrote him an avuncular note: "You certainly have tapped into a resource and a potential for good or for harm, depending on how it develops. You did it perhaps by chance at a time when the whole issue of religion, government and ideology [is] at the top of our national agenda. It should be clear to you that I have had my difficulties with anything other than normal associations with those with whom you are in close contact"— a veiled reference not only to Falwell and Robertson, but the Likud Party in Israel, with whom Klutznick had been feuding over the Palestinian issue. "You may have a point, but I have not convinced myself completely that your talents are being used in the best area that could promise the greatest results. It must be your enthusiasm that causes you to see possibilities which have escaped many of us." Enclosed was a check for $1,000—a significant donation by Eckstein's standards.

Things had picked up since the first lean year—in 1984, the Fellowship took in $122,898 and Eckstein's salary rose to $48,000—but while he could now pay the rent for his office, and meet his mortgage payments at home, there wasn't much of an operational budget. There was just enough for Eckstein to travel to churches and conventions, get booked on small Christian TV and radio shows, and try to spread his message. None of that required more than a salary, a small office, and some economy-class plane fares.

During this period, Klutznick was increasingly impressed by the young rabbi's ability to connect with "the extreme right of Christianity." By 1987, skepticism had turned to something like admiration.

"It is important," Klutznick wrote, "that what you are doing be kept alive. I may not agree with every aspect of it but then who does agree with every aspect of a tender and difficult situation?" This note, like the others, came with a check.

That year, Nate Perlmutter died and was replaced by Abe Foxman. Perlmutter had been Eckstein's patron at the ADL and remained a strong supporter. In 1985, the Fellowship had come under attack by liberal Jewish groups for its contacts with Falwell and Robertson, but Perlmutter warmly endorsed its work. "The Holyland Fellowship of Christians and Jews is an important bridge between evangelicals and Fundamentalists, and Jews," he wrote in a widely publicized statement. "For too long we have been strangers to each other. We both deserve better and the Fellowship is serving the creative purpose of understanding. That's the first, necessary ingredient of small 'f' fellowship."

Abe Foxman didn't share Perlmutter's warm regard for Eckstein. They clashed after Eckstein publicly criticized his old organization for perpetuating itself and, at times, stimulating fund-raising by drumming up unwarranted concerns over anti-Semitism. Foxman chastised Eckstein for betraying his former colleagues. The two men didn't speak for several years. It was only a crisis in Jewish-evangelical relations a few years later that renewed what remained a fraught relationship between the two.

While Foxman was fuming in New York, Eckstein invited Pat Robertson to the Standard Club, Chicago's premier "Jewish" city club, for a meeting with community leaders. Robertson was on the cusp of announcing his run for the Republican nomination for president. His main opponent, George H. W. Bush, was considered an uncertain friend of the Jews, because of his close ties to Middle Eastern oil countries. Robertson saw the possibility of raising money among the wealthy Jewish Republicans in the Windy City, some of whom were founders of the Fellowship. At the meeting, Robertson reminded the audience that in the 1982 Lebanon War, he had personally broadcast pro-Israeli reports from the battlefield on his Christian Broadcasting Network: "I swore an oath before the Lord that I and the organization I head would stand firmly with Israel and the Jewish people, no matter how difficult or unpopular it would be." Robertson also told the group that he supported the Holyland Fellowship, an endorsement that prompted Eckstein to explain, in his next bulletin, that while he appreciated the support, the Fellowship did not endorse any candidate for political office.

Of all Eckstein's Christian mentors, it is possible that Robertson was the most influential. Robertson invited him to come to Virginia Beach to appear on *The 700 Club* TV talk show. "We met before the show. I told him I had just read his book *Shout It From the Housetops!* and that I was in awe of what he had built. I asked him how he had done it. He said, 'It was all God's doing.' And then he said, 'Yechiel, I believe God is in your work and I will pray for your success. I want to be part of it and I will pray for you.' I remember walking out of that meeting feeling distraught and discouraged. Here I was without a full-time secretary or a real salary and all I was going to get from him was moral support. I needed money and he had it, but I didn't ask. I didn't have the temerity, although I felt that I had missed an opportunity. But when I got back to my office in Chicago, there was an envelope waiting for me. I opened it and found a personal check for $10,000 and a note from Pat: 'Yechiel, I want to walk with you on this.'"

It was the beginning of a long relationship that played a key role in realizing Eckstein's vision. "From the first time we met, I saw Yechiel as an extraordinarily attractive young man with a heart for reconciliation between Jews and Christians," says Robertson. "I had been trying to build bridges to the Jewish community for years, and he was doing the same thing. And I don't know of anyone who has done this more effectively."

Robertson knew he was disliked by the Jewish establishment. He was guilty of two sins: being a conservative minister on the wrong side of social and cultural issues, and being a Republican politician. "I understand that there is a suspicion about Christians, especially after World War II. And American Jews have an undying loyalty to the New Deal and the Democratic Party." But Robertson professes to be unconcerned. "My mother raised me on Genesis 12:3. God blesses those who bless his people, and gives the land to the people of Israel. That's scripture, simple as that," he said.

In the early years, it was Eckstein's Jewish supporters who kept the Fellowship afloat. They saw him as a scout in enemy territory, who could keep an eye on the goyim, the Gentiles, and issue an advance warning of trouble. Eckstein had an entirely different purpose. He believed he could touch Christian hearts and build a true fellowship. Visiting churches was fine, but retail recruiting was exhausting, especially because he was delivering a new and in some ways startling message. His guest appearances on *The 700 Club* and other Christian talk shows were successful but sporadic. What he needed was more airtime. That's where Jerry Rose came in.

Rose was one of the pioneers of evangelical television, starting his first station in Dallas. In 1976, he came to WCFL in Chicago, and at first he struggled in the city, with its small evangelical community and huge proportion of Catholics. He realized that the best way to grow the station was to leaven its hard-core fundamentalist message with ecumenism. He met with priests, mainline ministers, and rabbis, spreading the word that he wasn't up to some nefarious media campaign against them. As a Pentecostal, he had a special interest in connecting with the Jews, but it was a slippery journey. He ran a program called *The Jewish Voice*, which was produced by a missionary group that targeted Jews. When Yechiel, acting for the ADL, complained, Rose offered him airtime for ADL material. Rose also attached a disclaimer to the show, announcing that it was "*a* Jewish voice, but not *the* Jewish voice."

The two men struck up a friendship, and when Eckstein began thinking about setting up his own group, Rose advised him on the steps that might be necessary for effective bridge building. He also agreed to join the Fellowship's board of directors. Just as Bailey Smith had opened the doors to Southern Baptist churches, Rose gave Yechiel entrée to the National Religious Broadcasters, which

Rose went on to head, and the Pentecostal world. "Back then, people at the NRB conventions were surprised to bump into a guy wearing a yarmulke," Eckstein says. "Nowadays there are so many Jews at the convention I'll be walking down the hall and hear people calling out, 'We need a *minyan* for *mincha*' [a quorum for afternoon prayers]."

Eckstein and Rose were clear from the start about their boundaries. "I am an evangelical Christian, which means that I evangelize," Rose said. "If we can work together on that basis, great. But you have to understand, we can't say we want to save everybody but Jews. Evangelism is based on the premise 'whosoever will.'" Eckstein understood; in fact, it fit his own synthesis, reconciling "witnessing" and opposing "proselytizing." With Rose's help, Eckstein began appearing more frequently on Christian television. He also began a nationally syndicated radio program, *Ask the Rabbi.* Through the show, Eckstein invited evangelicals not just to learn more about Judaism, but also to regard him as their personal rabbi. For the first time, he began receiving donations from evangelicals: small checks, many made out to him directly, often with a letter thanking him for the opportunity to bless the Jewish people.

Even as Eckstein's ministry began to connect Jews and Christians, it refrained from holding interfaith gatherings. This was largely a protective measure. He knew from personal experience the emotional power of evangelical prayer, and he was concerned that it would prove overpowering to Jews. "I personally was never tempted to become a Christian. I'm too Jewish for that. I have a bellyful of *shas* and *poskim* [Torah learning and rabbinical legal training], but I knew how moving and seductive Christianity could be to Jews who don't have my background or piety."

He had been aware of this from his first visit to the Vineyard, in Orange County, California. Eckstein had come west to meet evangelicals who might be interested in the Fellowship. One such kindred soul took him to Sunday night services. "I was shocked," Eckstein says. "I had never been in a church that had a band on the pulpit. An electric guitar, drums, a rock band with a singing preacher. It cast a spell. The church was full of young people who seemed rapt, eyes closed in prayer, hands held up to God. Of course, I couldn't sing with them. Their prayers weren't mine. And wearing a yarmulke, I certainly stood out. I felt awkward. But I was also moved. I became very much aware of the power of this kind of worship."

That awareness was sharpened when, soon afterward, Eckstein traveled to Grand Rapids, Michigan, to host a dialogue between Jewish and evangelical laypeople. The event was held in an Assemblies of God church. As it was ending, he saw a Pentecostal woman reach out and embrace a Jewish woman. "Please tell me how it feels to be one of God's chosen!" she begged. The Jew, an active member of the local Reform temple, was speechless. Then she stammered, "I've never even thought about that."

For Yechiel it was a moment of clarity. "Right there I realized that bringing ordinary Jews, with their rote prayers and superficial understanding of Judaism into contact with committed evangelicals was too dangerous," he recalls. "The Jews in the audience simply lacked the emotional and religious resources to communicate on the same level. I worried they could convert."

There were, obviously, Jews whose religious seriousness and conviction matched the evangelicals'; the problem was that they weren't ready to meet and discuss religion with Christians. And so it fell to Eckstein to be the intermediary, the Jewish side of the discussion, a bridge builder to the evangelical world, a teacher to the Gentiles. "Rabbi" is a synonym for "teacher," and if Christians wanted to call him that, he wouldn't shrink from the appellation. At the same time, he saw himself as their ambassador and advocate to a Jewish community that was suspicious of and unfriendly to evangelical Christianity.

ROOTS: *The Eckstein clan circa 1921. The woman seated on the right is Yechiel's grandmother. The baby on her lap is Yechiel's father.*

FULL CIRCLE: *Yechiel's parents immigrated to Israel in 2011. They were greeted at the airport by three generations of Ecksteins.* (Yossi Zamir)

BAR MITZVAH: *Yechiel's trip to Israel, in 1964, was a bar mitzvah gift from his parents. He would have preferred a football helmet and a new bike.*

POWER FORWARD:
Yechiel in his Yeshiva High School days. Twice he played in Madison Square Garden.

THE WEDDING SINGER: *For years Yechiel made a good part of his living onstage, as a singer and band leader at Jewish events.*

TURNING POINT: *With Pat Boone (center) and Jack Hayford (left) at the IFCJ's first successful telethon.*

THE RABBI AND THE REVEREND: *Yechiel with Jerry Falwell making a joint telecast from Liberty University.*

CHRISTIAN MENTORS: *Yechiel with Pat Robertson* (center) *and Pat Boone* (right).

JOELLE AND YECHIEL ECKSTEIN:
"I prayed to God to send me a ten. And here she is." (Ronny Inc.)

THE ECKSTEIN DAUGHTERS:
Tamar, Yael, and Talia, in 2013.

MAN ON A MISSION:
Yechiel visited China and interceded with the government on behalf of Christian dissidents.

PARTNERS:
The relationship between IFCJ and Chabad has revolutionized Jewish charity in the former Soviet Union.

YECHIEL AND ARIEL: *Eckstein served as informal adviser to Sharon on Christian affairs and helped cement relations between Israel and the evangelical community.*

YECHIEL AND BIBI: *With Prime Minister Benjamin Netanyahu in Jerusalem. Eckstein and the IFCJ have a nonpartisan policy of working with every Israeli government.*

WITH THE TROOPS:
Yechiel was disappointed that he was too old to join the army when he moved to Israel. "You'll be more valuable as a civilian," the prime minister told him.
(Oren Nachshon)

WARTIME:
Inspecting rocket damage with the chief Ethiopian spiritual leader of Ashkelon, in 2012, on the Gaza border. (Olivier Fitoussi)

"WE LOVED YOU BEFORE YOU WERE BORN":
In an Odessa school in 2014. Later that year the IFCJ began airlifting refugees from the fighting in Ukraine to Israel.
(Moshe Bukhman)

THE JOURNEY HOME:
Eckstein gave thanks at the Wailing Wall in Jerusalem shortly after moving to Israel.

Six

❖

"QUESTIONABLE"

In the Orthodox world, studying Torah is a lifelong pursuit, a high act of piety and community solidarity. All over the world, tens of thousands of Jewish men past the age of formal education absorb the complete Talmud—the main object of study—a page a day, in seven-and-a-half-year cycles known as *daf yomi*, or daily page. The Talmud is a complex and difficult text, full of sophisticated legal reasoning and arcane rabbinical disputes. To master it you need complete fluency not only in Hebrew but also in Aramaic.

In 1988, Yechiel enrolled in the Chicago Community Kollel—a center for Torah study—in Rogers Park. His Kollel studies imposed a new burden on an already brutal schedule. At the Fellowship, Eckstein got to his desk by eight in the morning and often stayed well past eight at night; now he also had class six days a week, from 5:30 to 6:30 a.m., followed by forty-five minutes of prayer. But it was a fulfillment of his religious obligation that offered intellectual stimulation, the chance to deepen his knowledge and to be among peers. Like him, his fellow students were part of the Orthodox elite, men with strong Jewish backgrounds and motivation. Some held rabbinical degrees; others were doctors, lawyers, and pious businessmen—all *balebatishe lamdanim* like Yechiel's ancestor Simcha Bunam Eckstein. Yechiel's rabbinical training made him a star pupil, and his outgoing nature won him friends. The rabbis and students at the Kollel knew, at least in general terms, about his activities at the Fellowship.

In 1991, the Holyland Fellowship renamed itself the International Fellowship of Christians and Jews. The change, which was made without public comment or explanation, was a response to two concerns. Some of the Jewish board members thought that "Holyland" sounded too goyish; some of the evangelicals thought it sounded too Catholic. The new name was clunky, but it represented a truth, even if it wasn't completely apparent at the time.

That year, Eckstein moved to step up his public profile by producing and starring in a series of five-minute television spots called *Shalom from Israel*. Money for the series was fronted by four Jewish backers—Robert Lappin, Helen and Norman Asher, and Suzanne Peyser. Each episode began with a quotation from scripture, and then Eckstein explained how the passage related to present-day topics, ranging from the Feast of Tabernacles celebration in Jerusalem to the impact of the recent US invasion of Iraq, in which Iraqi Scud missiles were fired on Tel Aviv and Haifa. The shows linked

Eckstein and the Fellowship with the Jewish state, and the Jewish state with the Bible. Eckstein had been on Christian talk shows over the years, but this series demonstrated that he was telegenic enough to connect with a Christian audience on his own.

"I remember one episode whose theme was 'the desert shall bloom like a rose.' We focused on Israeli agricultural advances—drip irrigation and hydroponics, growing vegetables in hothouses. To do it we went to Susia, a settlement in the West Bank. It was the first time I ever visited a settlement and had to go in an armored car. We filmed, and on the way back we were attacked by a gang of rock-throwing kids. Arabs surrounded the car, rocked it from side to side, beating the windows and me screaming at the driver to get out of there. Here I was doing a film about growing strawberries, showing how Israel was fulfilling biblical texts, and I realized that yes, you can have the Bible and the fulfillment of prophecy, but the question is: How do you do it when you are dealing with Arabs who don't want you there?"

In the early days of the Fellowship, Eckstein led a trip to the Holy Land with Pat Boone, on behalf of the Christian Broadcasting Network. The two men discovered they had a lot in common. They were both singers, although Eckstein's religious recordings weren't in the same league as Boone's dozens of charted hits, which included "The Exodus Song" (with his lyric "God gave this land to me"). They were both ex-hoopsters too; Boone once played on a Hollywood team that included Bill Cosby. Boone had a BA from Columbia University, class of '58. Eckstein had been there almost two decades later. Most important, they were both ardent Zionists. Like Eckstein,

Boone had entertained troops in the Yom Kippur War, where he was bemused to discover that Israeli soldiers wanted to hear "Speedy Gonzales" more than "The Exodus Song."

Eckstein was flattered to be associated with Boone. "He was a Hollywood star to me." He also admired Boone's daughter Debby. "She had just come out with 'You Light Up My Life.' She agreed to cohost a series of radio programs with me on Israel and Jewish dialogue. Pat and Debby and I talked for years about putting out an album, but nothing came of it."

In Eckstein, Boone found a religiosity and sincerity that matched his own. He dubbed the young rabbi "the guileless Israelite," borrowing Jesus's description of the biblical Nathanael. "I found his commitment very moving," says Boone. "One time he and I were scheduled to do an event together in Washington, DC. It was a Friday afternoon, and things were running long. Backstage he kept looking at his watch and fretting about not being able to get home to Chicago in time for the Sabbath. Finally he just got up and left." Boone knew that Eckstein had a performer's ego and dedication to the maxim that the show must go on. "Yechiel's just that strict about Jewish law," he says.

With the fall of the USSR in 1989, Russian Jews were free to leave for Israel. For religious Jews as well as evangelical Christians it was a miracle, a second Exodus, and the fulfillment of biblical prophecies about the return of Jews to the Land of Israel from the four corners of the earth. The Israeli government saw it as a historic opportunity. By 2000, more than a million Jews had emigrated from the former

Soviet Union to Israel. They made an incalculable contribution to the country's security, economy, and self-confidence. Eighty years before, Communism and Zionism had vied for the hearts and minds of the Jews of Russia and Eastern Europe. For decades, the Soviet Union made the competition moot by locking its Jews behind the Iron Curtain. Now, given a choice, they were streaming into Israel. Jewish history was being made on the grandest possible scale, and Eckstein, who had been protesting against Soviet policies toward the Jews since his student days, was determined to play a part. In 1990, he and the Fellowship launched a new project, On Wings of Eagles, to help support the *aliyah*—literally the ascent—of Jews from Russia to Israel.

The idea caught the imagination of the evangelical public. By 1992, contributions to the Fellowship had increased almost threefold from the previous year, to $717,000. For the first time most of the funds were coming from Christians, who saw the Russian migration as a biblical exodus. There were similarities; one was that, as in the first Exodus, many of those departing slavery for the Promised Land were not actually Hebrews. After seventy years of Communism, a large percentage of the Russian Jews weren't actually Jewish, according to rabbinical law. But under Israel's Law of Return, they were eligible if they had at least one Jewish grandparent, and what was good enough for the Israeli government was good enough for the Fellowship.

Eckstein understood the moment, and its meaning for evangelical-Jewish cooperation. Fundamentalist Christians who longed to gain God's favor by blessing the people of Israel now had an opportunity to do so by helping to pay for their return to Zion. They saw it as biblical work, with the evidence right there in the book of Ezekiel: "Then they will know that I am the Lord their God, for though I sent them into exile among the nations, I will gather them to their own land, not leaving any behind." Those who helped the exiles return would be partnering with God.

To communicate this message, Eckstein turned to Boone. Robert Gottstein, an Alaskan Jewish businessman, staked the Fellowship to $28,000 to make a film and stage a telethon, called *While the Door Is Still Open*, which aired on the Family Channel and Christian television networks around the country in 1992. Boone hosted pro bono, bringing professionalism and star quality to the telecast; Jerry Falwell and Pat Robertson also agreed to make an appearance.

The telethon opened with footage of joyful Jews arriving at Israel's Ben Gurion Airport, as a chorus on the sound track sings, "We are leaving Mother Russia. When they come for us we'll be gone." The message is clear: Jews are fleeing the danger just in time, as they failed to do during the Holocaust. Boone came on the screen and explained that the people at the airport were escaping persecution in Russia and making a new life in the Promised Land. He called on viewers to save tens, maybe hundreds, of families. "We can make it happen as Christians," he said. "I am my brother's keeper. God is calling his children back home." For those who wanted to make their own call, there was an 800 number.

A young man and his father appeared and talked about Russian anti-Semitism, as file footage showed scenes of violence and discrimination against Jews. "Two million Jews fear that the demonic forces of anti-Semitism will be released again," a narrator intoned.

"We've been given a second chance to save the Jewish people," said Boone. Citing the book of Jeremiah, he said, "It is God's plan for the ingathering of the Jews to the Land of Israel, from the 'land of the north'"—which, in evangelical English, is widely understood as a reference to Russia.

Falwell appeared on the screen. He said, "God is bringing about an incredible prophecy," and praised the International Fellowship of Christians and Jews for enabling Christians to take part. After him came Pastor Jack Hayford, leader of the International Church of the Foursquare Gospel, who identified himself as a member of the IFCJ and declared that partnering with the Fellowship was partnering in the fulfillment of prophecy, "something God would have me do." Robertson completed the trifecta of endorsements. He made his own appeal for contributions to the Fellowship and declared that "we will see the time of fulfillment, the reign of the Messiah."

By the time Eckstein appeared on-screen, it was time to get down to cases. He quietly informed the audience that it would cost $2.3 billion to bring Jews to Israel over the next three years. He called on Christian "brothers and sisters" for help, and put the price of transporting and settling each Jew at $600. The audience was invited to contact On Wings of Eagles.

Boone closed the show by calling on Christians to donate "fifty dollars, two hundred and fifty, whatever you can afford." It was an unprecedentedly large ask for Christian television, and intentionally so. It was meant to signal the magnitude of the task and of the moment. The chorus of voices once again chanted, "We are leaving Mother Russia," as Boone ended the broadcast by reciting God's promise from Genesis 12:3. The next day, money began flowing in undreamed-of amounts.

In those days, Eckstein made a practice of flying down to Virginia Beach every few months to breakfast with Pat Robertson. On his first visit after the telethon, he reported that it was bringing in money at more than double the industry standard. For every dollar spent, the Fellowship took in $2.30. Robertson was certain that Eckstein was mistaken, but there was no mistake. The small staff at the Fellowship was having a hard time even processing all the donations. Eckstein, who had made a practice of thanking every donor personally, found himself unable to keep up. Within two years of the first broadcast of the telethon, enough had come in to underwrite the aliyah—the immigration to Israel—of a thousand Jews from Russia as well as $100,000 to pay for the immigration of Ethiopian Jews.

Eckstein's Fellowship was succeeding. He was becoming known and respected in the evangelical world. He was donating money to Israel. People were paying attention. And soon, that became a problem.

In 1991, the *Chicago Tribune* ran an article on Eckstein. Titled "Rabbi's Mission an Unusual Mix," the story described his ecumenical activities over the past dozen years, his many friendships among fundamentalist Christians, and his basic operational philosophy of "cooperate where possible, oppose when necessary and sensitize and teach at all times." The reporter, Michael Hirsley, noted that Eckstein's activities had led him through minefields of misunderstanding but that they were now the subject of "minimal controversy." Toward the end of the story he described the young rabbi's indefatigable energy, "waking at five a.m. to study the Torah and jog before work." Hirsley was unaware that this seemingly innocuous piece of information was about to detonate the biggest mine of Eckstein's career.

Shortly afterward, Eckstein came to class at the Kollel and realized that no one was looking him in the eye. "I realized at the time that some eyebrows might be raised because it mentioned that I visited Reform temples, although I made it clear that I didn't pray there. But that wasn't it. Finally the teacher said, 'We saw the story in the paper. It's creating a problem.'" There had been no mention of the particular kollel, but there weren't many such places in the Chicago area and people figured it out quickly. Eckstein was called to the office of the headmaster and grilled about what exactly he was up to. What was he teaching? Who was he teaching it to? Who gave him permission to go into churches? Yechiel was taken aback; he had discussed the Fellowship with the headmaster in the past, and no objections had been raised. But that was before the whole city— the whole world!—had been informed.

The headmaster said, "There is a question about whether you can be here, in the Kollel."

"Are you saying there is a question about whether I am permitted to learn Torah?" Eckstein asked. In the Orthodox world, being questionable is a short step from being excommunicated.

The rosh yeshiva nodded.

"I panicked," says Eckstein. "All I could think about was Spinoza being excommunicated. I asked why this was happening."

The rosh yeshiva said that Yechiel might be in violation of the commandment that forbids teaching Torah to goyim. A rabbinical court made up of prominent American rabbis would have to be convened. The rabbis would be drawn from Agudat Yisrael, the umbrella party of the ultra-Orthodox movement. Eckstein would have to appear as a defendant. The move was so extreme that, even now, no one there can recall a similar proceeding. Very likely it was unprecedented.

For perhaps the first time in his life, Eckstein rebelled. At Columbia, his doctoral thesis had been on the question of religious authority. All his life he had submitted to it. When his father told him to go to yeshiva, he went. When he had been challenged at Tamar's bat mitzvah, he had simply buried his head in his prayer shawl. But this was too much. He informed the headmaster that he would not go before a rabbinical court and be forced to prove his Jewish credentials. "If you have a question about me, go ahead and ask the rabbis," he said. "But I refuse to appear. I won't go."

"Fine," said the rosh yeshiva. "But you understand that you won't be welcome here until the case is decided. Consider yourself suspended for the next thirty days."

During that month, Eckstein discovered that he had become a *cause célèbre*. From Chicago to New York and all the way to Jerusalem, Orthodox Jews were debating his case. Ancient black-hat rabbinical judges who had never met an evangelical—and who barely tolerated the sort of Judaism Yechiel had learned in the modern Orthodox institutions of his youth—deliberated on his kosher bona fides as though he was an improperly slaughtered chicken. He felt uncomfortable even walking into a synagogue, where he knew he would be the object of stares and whispers. But he needed a place to pray, now more than ever.

An old friend from Ottawa told him about a small shul where he would certainly be welcome. Relieved, he went there on Shabbat, and came home feeling grateful. The next day the friend called. "I don't know how to tell you this," he said, "but the rabbi asked me to let you know that he would prefer if you didn't come back. He said you are 'questionable.'" Yechiel hung up and felt a chill.

At the end of the thirty-day period, Eckstein received a phone call from Rabbi David Cohen, one of the judges. He and one other judge, Rabbi Avraham Pam, had voted to exonerate him. The other two found him guilty. As in baseball, the tie went to the runner; he could return to class, be a Jew among Jews, and once again be allowed to study Torah. He was still kosher, but barely.

Yechiel received the decision with anger and sadness. A tie vote might have sufficed for the Kollel—although it was made clear to him that nobody would be sorry if he didn't return—but for him it was another humiliation. He called Rabbi Cohen back and said, "Without a four to zero verdict, I don't feel I can lift my head in public."

Cohen urged Eckstein to return. He, after all, had advocated for him, and if Eckstein didn't resume his studies it could be viewed as disrespectful. Eckstein saw the point. "I felt I had to go back because I had at least been given status quo ante. I owed it to him." When he walked into class, the teacher refused to acknowledge his presence. His classmates stared at him blankly. At the end of the class, he didn't come back. But he was too stubborn to drop his Talmudic studies. Finishing the *daf yomi* cycle is the Jewish equivalent of getting through the Ironman competition, and he was determined to get to the finish line. For that he needed to find a place that would have him.

He found it at a Chabad synagogue not far away. The teacher, Rabbi Yosef Bechhofer, was a young man who had grown up in West Hempstead and knew Bonnie's parents. He also knew the story of the previous Kollel. "I was aware that Yechiel had written a book and said some positive things about Jesus," Bechhofer says. He went to his boss, Rabbi Zvi Shusterman, and asked for guidance. Shusterman said that Yechiel would be welcome. "I knew Rabbi Shusterman and he knew me," says Eckstein. "He felt bad about what I had gone through at Tamar's bat mitzvah, at a Chabad shul. Shusterman was a more normative Chabad rabbi, open and welcoming. Maybe he even wanted me to see that not all Chabad rabbis are as rigid and self-righteous as the one I ran into at the bat mitzvah. Anyway, he decided to give me a chance."

Eckstein came to class that first day in a state of trepidation. He was afraid that someone would object to his presence, but no one did. He quickly became, once again, the star pupil. "If Yechiel had wanted to go that way, he would have been a great Talmud scholar," says Rabbi Bechhofer. "He's very smart, and he asked a lot of tough questions. Some teachers don't like questions. I do." Bechhofer was interested in Christian theology, and Eckstein found himself conducting a tutorial. "I remember asking him: If Christian salvation depends entirely on accepting Jesus, what is the need for good works? Yechiel explained that if the acceptance was actually sincere, Christians believed, it would naturally lead to good works. I found it very interesting."

Eckstein remained at the Kollel for three more years and completed the cycle. "I had completed what I had started, despite all the pain and the difficulties. Frankly, I was very proud of myself," he says.

When he was done with the cycle, he stopped going to shul on a regular basis. The rush and rote of prayer in many synagogues was unfulfilling. He wanted to take his time and actually feel the experience. "This is what's called *kavanah*, proper intention in prayer," he says.

Synagogues were also a place where he knew that some of his fellow Jews considered him a pariah. He had the feeling he was being observed and gossiped about. That happened not just in Chicago and New York; his reputation as "questionable" preceded him everywhere. "I was in Argentina, and I went to a synagogue on Shabbat," he recalls. "The rabbi gave me the honor of saying a public blessing over the Torah. After services, a man approached him and complained. He had heard that I was a Christian missionary. Incidents like that—and they were frequent—gave me the feeling that I am radioactive. I began to feel queasy going to shul in most places."

It made him even more uneasy to admit that he felt more spiritually alive in some of the evangelical churches he visited than in synagogues. He began to *daven* at home, praying by himself in the backyard. He still said the standard morning prayers, as he had all his life, but he said them alone, and he began to tinker with them around the edges. For example, he no longer thanked God for not making him a goy; instead, he expressed thanks for being made a Jew. And he also dropped the prayer thanking God for not making him a woman. He was a rabbi with daughters, after all.

"Just being able to address God personally, to say 'Baruch atah [Blessed are you]' to the creator of the universe, was thrilling to me." Alone in his yard, he could commune with nature, reflect on the words of the traditional prayers, and pray at his own pace. "I've had many great moments with God, but there was *one* time, sitting in the yard on the patio, when I was one with the universe. I've never had such a strong feeling again, such a sense of oneness with God and creation."

Eckstein never lost faith in the God of Israel or the Jewish people. But he did lose faith in the religious communities and institutions that he had belonged to all his life. "I realized that among the conventionally Orthodox I would always be an oddball, a square peg," he says. "My ideal was still to be part of a minyan. As a rabbi, I recognize the implications of praying with a quorum and I go when I find a soulful one, a place my heart can soar. But the regular synagogue services often feel like just going through the motions with nine other men. That isn't meaningful to me."

Bonnie and the girls would see him on the patio, lost in prayer, his tallis (prayer shawl) over his head, weeping or singing or dancing, trying, as he had tried all his life, to become one with God. She found this disturbing. The man she had married had been a scholar, an entertainer, a charmer, a *catch*. She liked that he had gone outside the yeshiva world and held a graduate degree from an Ivy League school. She related easily to his work for the ADL; her father, after all, had spent his life in organizational Jewish pursuits. Like Yechiel, Bonnie was an observant Jew, but her vibe was modern, American, and liberal, and she thought his was too. She knew he was a spiritual seeker, a student of Buddhism. That didn't seem odd to her. She belonged to an American generation that appreciated the appeal of Eastern religion. What did seem odd, and disconcerting, was his interest in evangelical Christianity. It had been part of his job at the ADL, but the Fellowship was something different, threatening. She declined to play an active role as the founder's wife and didn't enjoy the interfaith gatherings at their home. "Yechiel invited me to his place for Shabbat dinner," says Lynn Doerschuk, an evangelical filmmaker who worked with him. "He wanted me to share the experience. Bonnie wasn't welcoming, put it that way. He told me that she didn't like the fact that he was becoming known as a person who works with Christians. That was a pretty common view in Chicago, among Orthodox Jews."

Yechiel wanted Bonnie to understand the beauty and power of

evangelical worship. On a visit to a Christian ministry in Puerto Rico that supported the Fellowship, she joined him at Sunday prayer service in the basement of the pastor's house. "I hoped she would understand me, see why I saw this as a Christian form of Hasidic worship—the sort of worship my soul was so passionate about. I hoped she would see why I needed emotional power in my own Jewish prayer. But she didn't. Bonnie said that it had been moving, but I felt she was simply saying that to make me happy." Ecstasy hadn't been what she was looking for in her own worship. And now, here was her husband, sitting outside on the patio in all sorts of weather, dancing and singing. It seemed fanatical to her and, well, goyish. "She thought that maybe I was out of my mind," says Yechiel.

There were other tensions in the marriage. Some revolved around money. Early in their marriage, Yechiel and Bonnie decided to buy their house in Skokie. Yechiel swallowed his pride and asked his father for a loan to help cover the down payment. Sy turned him down flat. Yechiel found the experience "emasculating" and vowed never to repeat it. He also didn't have the audacity to ask his father-in-law for help.

Instead, he took a new job as a weekend rabbi at a synagogue in Evanston. It was a forty-five-minute walk from Skokie, and he did it rain or shine, winter and summer. He went alone—Bonnie and the girls attended a large, modern Orthodox synagogue near the house—and he often didn't get back until three in the afternoon, too late to join the family for Shabbat lunch, a meal that had been the linchpin of his own boyhood. He ate alone and then, exhausted, went to his room to nap alone. As the Fellowship became more successful, Bonnie pressed Yechiel to take a larger salary. He was, after all, the one raising all the money, and it would enable him to spend more time with her and the girls. Yechiel resisted, saying that the evangelical donations were sacrificial, and he felt a duty to be a modest steward. Bonnie derided him for what she saw as vanity disguised as humility.

"My mother loved my father, but she had a very hard time with his need for outside validation," says his daughter Yael. "He'd come home and say, 'I was written up in this or that place' but she wasn't impressed by that. She'd say, 'Yes, but how did it make you feel? Tell me about you, not what other people said or wrote about you.' She didn't care about honors or publicity."

Yechiel cared—it was part of his work—but he also wanted to impress Bonnie, who, he felt, was constantly comparing him unfavorably with her father. The two men had never warmed to one another. "Never, in all the years we were married, did Henry ask me how things were with me, what I was doing. He had no interest at all in me or my work. Every conversation was about him."

As time went by, geopolitics became an issue. When Yechiel met Bonnie, Siegman was a conventional American Jewish apparatchik, but over the years he became critical and then openly hostile to the policies of successive Israeli governments. He began calling Israel an "apartheid state," blamed its settlement policies for many seemingly unrelated problems in the Middle East, castigated the Israel lobby in the United States, and advocated an Israeli withdrawal to the borders of the 1947 partition plan. He was vocal about his new positions and proud of the friends who came with them. He became friendly with Yasser Arafat. On one occasion, he called from a Saudi royal palace to wish his daughter and grandchildren a good Shabbat. Eckstein noted that in Saudi Arabia, it was already past dark, so the telephone call was a violation of the Sabbath.

Siegman also despised Christian Zionism, with its maximalist demands. When Yechiel defended the evangelicals, Siegman mocked him—and Bonnie remained silent. "Bonnie lionized him," says Eckstein. "I could never compete with him for her affection. Nothing that I did, no amount of acclaim could compete. We were in a competition for her love and I never stood a chance. My need for acknowledgment and publicity stemmed from my relationship with my father, no doubt. But it also came from her relationship with hers."

Another inheritance from his parents was a lack of confidence in his parental ability. "I grew up with the old-fashioned model that father knows best," he says. "The power should belong to the parents. But I didn't feel that way personally, and so I was sometimes confused about what to do. If the girls asked me simple questions, like 'Can I go to a friend's house?' I was uncertain, so I told them to ask their mother."

The Eckstein girls, now in their thirties, reflect different aspects of their father's personality. Tamar, the eldest, no longer remembers Yechiel's public humiliation at her bat mitzvah (although she recalls not being allowed to decorate with balloons) but she has his jaundiced view of Orthodox intolerance, stemming largely from her experiences in Orthodox day school. On one occasion she was sent home because her skirt was half an inch shorter than the school's prescribed limit. On another, a teacher informed her that girls who dress immodestly should expect to be raped. She reacted by rebelling and becoming alienated from Orthodox Judaism. When she married, in 2014, the ceremony was performed by Eckstein's old friend David Ellenson, one of America's leading Reform rabbis.

Talia, the middle daughter, inherited her father's musical talent and his athleticism. As a teenager she was a nationally ranked gymnast who might have made the US Olympic Team if she had been willing to compete on the Sabbath. Religion came naturally to her, and so did affection for her father. "When I was growing up I never really knew what he was building at work. He kept it separate from our home life. He'd come home late most nights, around ten, when we were in our rooms and our mother was already in bed. He'd come in and, especially if he'd been out of town, lay out junk food on the bed for us," she recalls. Bonnie didn't appreciate such violations of house rules, and let her daughters know it. "My mother condescended to him," Talia says. "My older sister, when she was a teenager, had issues that she took out on him. At Shabbat dinner I always sat on his lap. It was my way of signaling that if you mess with my dad, you mess with me." Sometimes she would go out on the patio while he was praying and marvel at how rapt he was, how hard he was trying to find comfort.

Yael was the baby, born around the time Yechiel founded the Fellowship. She was a mama's girl and, later, a bit of a wild child. In high school she was busted for smoking pot. "My dad and my mom came to the police station to get me out. She was furious. I had let her down, and she walked right past me to the desk to arrange my release. My dad just put his arms around me and hugged me."

Eckstein remembers the moment vividly. "I was never completely certain how to be a parent," he says. "I was raised in an old-fashioned, 'do as I say' style. I didn't want to raise kids that way, but I really didn't know how to relate to them other than just loving them and trying to make them feel secure. In a way it was a relief that I didn't have sons who would have seen me as a role model and who I would have felt obliged to teach and discipline."

In the winter of 1992, Yechiel suffered a serious blow when his friend and mentor Jamie Buckingham died. Buckingham was a Pentecostal minister from Melbourne, Florida, a columnist at *Charisma* magazine—one of the leading journals of evangelical life—and a member of the Fellowship's board of directors. Like Jerry Rose and Pat Robertson, he was a surrogate Christian father to Yechiel, and theirs was a mutual admiration society. In the last column he wrote before he died, Buckingham described Eckstein as "a brilliant young Orthodox rabbi" who was devoted to helping Jews and Christians understand one another. "In churches where he has spoken he is widely acclaimed. Others sneer and call him an 'unbeliever.' Yet he is a bridge builder . . . there is no higher calling."

Buckingham had been sick with cancer, but in the spring of 1991 he announced in his *Charisma* column that he had been cured by the power of Christian positive thinking. "The cancer was trying to have me, but the Word of God said I was healed through what Jesus did on Calvary." He had, he wrote, been listening to an Oral Roberts sermon when he felt God's presence. "I came up off the sofa, shouting, 'I'm healed!' My wife leaped out of her chair and shouted, 'Hallelujah!' For the next thirty minutes all we did was walk around the house shouting thanks to God."

Less than a year later, Buckingham was gone, and Yechiel was desolate. "Jamie's death was one of the hardest things I ever experienced," he says. "He *believed* in me. I guess he was the first to believe in me. Not Bonnie, my parents, my friends . . . he believed in me!"

At Buckingham's memorial service, Yechiel sang a psalm in English and Hebrew, but he was so emotional he was unable to read the eulogy he had written. After the service, he and John French, a follower of Buckingham's, sat and cried together. Eckstein fell into a depression that lasted for months. "I felt like a zombie," he recalls. "Sometimes I couldn't stop crying. Even getting out of bed was difficult. I felt abandoned, forsaken, and distant from God. It was a very, very frightening time."

And yet, while Eckstein languished, the Fellowship flourished, due to the power of television. *While the Door Is Still Open* was showing around the country, and money poured in. Not only that, there was plenty of material still in the can. Years later, when Eckstein was pressed by the board of directors, now headed by John French, about his plan for succession, he suggested—only half in jest—that there needn't be a succession. "Just keep running the infomercials and don't tell anyone I'm dead," he joked. "With reruns, nobody will even notice I'm gone."

Seven

❖

OVER TROUBLED WATERS

In May 1995, Eckstein flew to Colorado Springs to tape an interview for Focus on the Family's highly influential daily radio broadcast. The interview was conducted by Dr. James Dobson, the president of the group, and titled *Understanding Our Jewish Friends*. In late July, one of Dobson's producers wrote a note thanking Eckstein for sharing his "important message" and hoping that it would be "instrumental in bringing healing and greater understanding to those who hear it." This was a big deal. Over the years Eckstein had managed to form close relations with a number of the highest-profile evangelical figures in the country, but Dobson had been somewhat standoffish. Adding him to the list of Christian supporters of the Fellowship would carry weight.

Instead, in September, a few days before the scheduled broadcast,

Eckstein got a letter from Dobson informing him that he had decided to spike the interview due to a "major controversy" sparked by Eckstein's writings on the subject of Christian evangelism, in which the rabbi made it clear that he opposed efforts to missionize Jews. "We are commanded by Jesus, 'Go ye into the world and preach the gospel to every creature,'" Dobson wrote. "Apparently, you have argued against this obligation in some of your books and this has created a storm of protest about your appearance on our program. More than a hundred stations have refused to air the interview, and one large network has even implied that they will take us off the air permanently if we go through with this program. Under the circumstances, and after appealing to the Lord for wisdom, the decision has been made to delete the broadcast."

Eckstein, needless to say, was upset. He had sent out a notice to his donors about the appearance (at an expense, he pointed out in a letter to Dobson, of $838.00). More than that, he was concerned that the cancellation would have serious repercussions for his work in the evangelical world, and that Dobson seemed to have worrisome ideas about his positions. He informed Dobson that he was very much a supporter of Christians' right and duty to carry out the Great Commission to witness to the world. "The question is, *how* Christians ought to do so; whether they'll bang us over the head with the gospel (as was done with catastrophic results over the centuries) or sensitively present this 'good news' and then let God and the Holy Spirit bring about whatever change God will."

Eckstein believed that messianic Christian groups like Jews for Jesus were spreading a false narrative about him. "Dobson believed their campaign against him would lose him radio stations," he says. In his letter, though, Eckstein refrained from accusing Dobson of such a self-interested motive. He simply wrote back expressing his hope that the "distorted impression you were given not gain widespread acceptance." He also told Dobson that he felt the need to go public with the cancellation, with a number of "key friends" who had been made aware of the interview and who would wonder why it hadn't been broadcast. These friends, copied on the letter, were a who's who of evangelical leadership, including Falwell, Robertson, Hayford, Boone, Gary Bauer, Ralph Reed, Jimmy Draper, and Rich Buhler.

Dobson responded in a conciliatory tone. He acknowledged Eckstein's need to inform his supporters, and expressed regret that he had been forced to cancel the interview. "Let's not let Satan tear us apart and thwart our common purposes," he wrote. "There's too much at stake."

Eckstein realized that he had a serious problem. If messianic groups had the support of someone as influential as Dobson, it could jeopardize the Fellowship. He wrote back to Dobson, saying that the pressure to cancel his appearance was part of a campaign being waged against him by missionaries. "I am not asking you to do anything to counter this," he wrote. "I just wanted you to know, however, that your response to the unfounded and malicious charge made against me and this ministry (the first time such a charge has been given credence by anyone since the Holyland Fellowship was founded in 1983, let alone by a leader of your stature) apparently has spurred these folks on to the point of their trying to eliminate the entire Wings of Eagles program."

Once more, Dobson responded with praise for Eckstein's role as a peacemaker and prayers that God would shower him with the richest of blessings. But there was no apology for, or even recognition of, the role pressure groups had played in canceling his appearance. Dobson's letter was a brush-off, written in evangelical English.

Jews for Jesus is the most visible of the messianic Jews who have been Eckstein's critics and rivals in the evangelical community. The group was founded in 1973 in San Francisco by two converted Jews, Moishe Rosen and Jhan Moskowitz. There had been Christian missions to the Jews for decades—in 1923, the Moody Bible Institute in Chicago established a chair, the first of its kind in America, to explore ways of winning Jews for Christ. A Yiddish version of the New Testament was published, but it evidently lost something in translation. In those days the Jewish masses, whether they were Orthodox, secular, or atheist, resisted Christianity and steered clear of the missionaries. Socially ambitious Jews *did* convert to Christianity, but it wasn't to the hot stuff the evangelicals were peddling.

Jews for Jesus peddled old wine in new bottles. It came out of the hippie culture of San Francisco and spoke to baby boomers whose Jewish identity and religious traditions had been diluted in the melting pot of the fifties. The group portrayed Jesus as one of them, a Jewish dude with cool sandals who also happened to have superpowers. Rosen was a marketing genius—the name Jews for Jesus alone was worth a thousand headlines and magazine covers—and he had the support of many Southern Baptists.

The Fellowship and Jews for Jesus were on one another's radar screens early. From the start, Eckstein had been suspected by his fellow Jews of being a Christian secret agent. Jews for Jesus turned the charge on its head, accusing him of passing himself off as a Christian. They charged that he obscured the fact that he didn't accept Jesus by an adroit use of evangelical English. "My main problem with Yechiel Eckstein is that Christians in the pews believe that he is a messianic Jew," says the current head of the organization, David Brickner. "Everywhere I go, people tell me, 'I love what you do. I just donated to the International Fellowship of Christians and Jews.' I say, 'Do you know that Rabbi Eckstein doesn't believe in Jesus?' And they are shocked. Sometimes they start to cry. They don't know he isn't one of us—he is our opposition."

If they don't, it isn't Eckstein's fault. From the earliest days of the Fellowship he has gone out of his way, for reasons of his own self-interest, to make it clear that he does not consider himself a Christian. From time to time, when an overly enthusiastic pastor introduced him as a "former rabbi" or a follower of Jesus, he learned to correct such misunderstandings with clarity and humor, as he had at Bailey Smith's church when he deflected the offer to return for a crusade. To donors who called the Fellowship seeking clarification on positions, he provided his staff with directions on how to respond:

"Does the rabbi accept Jesus as Messiah?"

"The Rabbi is an Orthodox Jew, which means that he anticipates the coming of the Messiah. Rabbi Eckstein states in his book Five Questions Most Frequently Asked about Jews and Judaism *that more and more Jews see Jesus as a great moral teacher who was kind, loving and compassionate toward others. The Rabbi, who frequently teaches on Romans 9–11 (which alludes to this matter), views Jesus as in some way 'sent' by God to bring salvation to the Gentiles. This represents a fundamental shift from the hostile attitudes Jews have had toward Jesus and his ministry for centuries."*

"Does the Rabbi approve of evangelizing?"

"While we affirm the right and duty of evangelical Christians to share the gospel, our mission and purpose is not to convert people to either Christianity or to Judaism. There are other ministries—both Christian and Jewish—that include spreading their faith as part of their mission. Because of our unique position of bridging the gap that has existed between Christians and Jews for millennia, we focus our ministry efforts on blessing Israel and the Jewish people. As we respond to the physical needs of suffering Jews around the world, they know that the help they receive comes from Christians who love Israel and her people."

In *What Christians Should Know about Jews and Judaism*, Eckstein called messianic Jewish Christianity "a theological impossibility" and asserted that "a Jew who accepts Jesus spurns his faith, abandons his community, and forfeits his right to claim that he is acting Jewishly." He implored Christians to "to leave the conversion of Jews to God, who may or may not bring it about when the full time of the Gentiles arrives." This advice was not warmly received by Jews for Jesus. (It probably didn't help that Eckstein described the group as "pushy, overly aggressive, and conniving.") One of its leaders responded that taking advice from Yechiel Eckstein on the proper way to bring people to Jesus Christ "is like taking advice from Al Capone on how to pay your income tax."

Jews for Jesus was always more of a public relations success than a serious converter of Jews. But the group's aggressive use of Jewish religious symbols and language drew lots of media attention. The group was also promoted by the hard-liners of the Southern Baptist Convention, who saw Eckstein's ministry, and his synthesis, as a means of weakening the Great Commission.

Eckstein was, of course, aware of this. As early as 1984, he publicly warned the Southern Baptist leadership that messianic missionaries were "a major source of potential discord between evangelical Christians . . . and Jews." One arena of that discord was Israel. In 1999, ultra-Orthodox members of the Israeli parliament proposed a bill that would criminalize missionary activity. It was a gratuitous provocation. Israel already prohibited missionaries from offering material inducement to someone to change religion, or approaching minors without the permission of their parents. The proposed new law was much tougher; it made missioning illegal and penalized it with up to nine years in prison.

Eckstein vehemently opposed and lobbied against it. In a protest to the Israeli embassy, he called the legislation "a travesty that would effectively prohibit both free speech and the free exercise of religion."

The legislative initiative ultimately failed, but it did damage. The following year, the Southern Baptist Convention reaffirmed its mission to proselytize the Jews, and called upon its members to pray for their conversion during the High Holidays period. Abe Foxman wrote a long letter of protest to Paige Patterson, the head of the SBC, accusing the group of "arrogance" and of creating the sort of atmosphere that "prepared the way for the Pagan anti-Semitism of the Holocaust." Patterson replied in a letter. "One Jew"—he meant Jesus—"told me that we are to pray that all men everywhere, especially His own ethnic people, would come to Christ. . . . Another Jewish theologian whom we greatly respect"—Saint Paul—"has stated that the gospel is 'for the Jew first and then also to the Gentile.' Another Jew"—Foxman—"now tells me that we ought not to do these things and that they are offensive. Therefore I am caught in a terrible bind between Jewish groups. . . . I really have no choice but to follow the advice of the Jew who died for me on the cross." Patterson also pointedly noted that the Southern Baptists strongly support religious liberty and pluralism in America, positions that benefit the Jewish community in particular.

As part of their call to mission, Patterson announced a plan to send a large contingent of missionaries to Chicago. A group of interfaith leaders, including Eckstein, wrote and asked him to reconsider. After the request was leaked to the media, Patterson objected that the move was meant to "intimidate" him, and insisted that the missionaries would indeed come "as men and women of peace." This was the greatest single challenge to the Eckstein doctrine of passive "witness" since the start of the Fellowship.

Eckstein had known Patterson for twenty years, and considered him a friend, but he felt that he was being unreasonable. He told the *New York Times* that the Baptist resolution "clearly crossed the line, from general evangelizing and witnessing—which I strongly affirm— and breached the trust" of Jewish-evangelical understanding. Patterson responded that the Southern Baptists were "targeting nobody specifically" and that the mandate was to "bring the gospel to the whole world, including the Jews."

Eckstein's ministry had, in a sense, begun with his friendship with Bailey Smith, the former head of the Southern Baptist Convention whose "moderates" had been ousted by Patterson's hard-line faction. Their congregations were an important part of his ministry. But he couldn't align himself with a faction that wanted to send an army of missionaries to Chicago, of all places, to knock on Jewish doors for Christ. He wrote to Patterson, informing him that he and the Fellowship of Christians and Jews were forced to suspend relations with the largest Protestant denomination in America. Patterson dismissed this as posturing, and asserted that only one of every five thousand contacts would be a Jew. But he made no apology. Instead, he cited Saint Paul's dictum, calling missionary work "the very breath of God." Patterson also expressed disappointment at the "incredible antagonism that Jews felt toward fellow Jews who had embraced Jesus as the

Messiah." Patterson concluded his letter to Eckstein by inviting him to "go right ahead and break relations with Southern Baptists if you wish. It does not change our loyalty and love for Jews. It does not change my personal love and appreciation for you." He admonished Eckstein to follow the example of the ancient Gamaliel, who—according to the New Testament book of Acts—counseled the Jewish leaders of his time to "keep away from these [Christian] men and leave them alone; for if this plan or this work is of men, it will come to nothing; but if it is of God you cannot overthrow it—lest you even be found to be fighting against God."

Eckstein had taken one of the biggest gambles of his career. Southern Baptists made up a considerable part of his organizational support and alienating them for a religious principle would have cost him and his organization dearly. But the bridge-building work he had done over the years paid off. Jerry Falwell and Pat Robertson stood up for him with the Baptists. Even more important, Billy Graham came to his aid. "I normally defend my denomination," he told a Fox News interviewer. "I'm loyal to it. But I have never targeted Muslims. I have never targeted Jews." In the end, the army of missionaries never arrived and Patterson let the initiative die.

Still, relations with the Southern Baptist Convention were never fully restored. Its churches no longer invited Eckstein to appear, nor did they take part in joint programs. "I grew a little disillusioned. I asked myself, What is the point of friendships and relationships if something like this happens?" But by now his evangelical support didn't depend on gatekeepers. His television infomercials appealed to Christian Zionists regardless of their denomination, and there were more than enough pastors in the Assemblies of God, and in other Charismatic and Pentecostal churches, who were delighted to offer him a place on the pulpit.

One of the most important was Jack Hayford, the founder of the Church On the Way, a Pentecostal megachurch in the San Fernando Valley in Los Angeles and one of evangelical America's most influential figures. He and Eckstein met for the first time in the early 1980s, at a Christian Booksellers Convention in Atlanta, and the two grew close. He played a key role in endorsing the Fellowship and in the success of the Wings of Eagles program, inviting Eckstein to appear at a conference of the International Church of the Foursquare Gospel in California to deliver a greeting and pass out material on the need to bring Jews back to Israel.

Hayford became one of Eckstein's Christian father figures, along with Pat Robertson, John French, *Christian Life* magazine founder Robert Walker, and Jamie Buckingham. Reverend Hayford saw the young rabbi, so full of sincerity and energy, as a surrogate son. Hayford had been to the Holy Land many times, but he hadn't had much of a connection to modern Israel or American Jews. Now, through Eckstein, he was able to become part of the miracle that he was certain was taking place after the fall of the Soviet empire. "Everything was birthed in that atmosphere," he says. "It was the start of the Wings of Eagles."

Hayford's Zionism was rooted in his interpretation of the Bible. "I don't believe that Jesus came to start Christianity, he came to fulfill God's covenant with the Jews. In John, Jesus said: 'Salvation is of the Jews.' I consider myself a descendant of King David and his seed. And because of that I have an unto-death commitment to Israel." Like Falwell, Robertson, and Graham, he was prepared to follow Eckstein's prescription for proper evangelism. "I see the Jews as God's chosen people and I don't argue with the Almighty," he says. "I believe in making good works my witness for Jesus. I think the nature of God requires good manners. I'd be martyred before I took part in or supported a forced or coerced conversion."

Not all the disputes between evangelical leaders and Jewish organizations were theological. At a rally in Virginia, Jerry Falwell told the crowd, "I know a few of you here today don't like Jews. And I know why. [They] can make more money accidentally than you can on purpose. I want to stand with the Jews. If that's where God blesses, I want to stand close." Falwell meant well, but it sounded wrong. At Eckstein's urging, he had his organization, the Moral Majority, take out a full-page newspaper ad, stating that many members were committed to the Jewish people for religious reasons, and that supporting Israel was a condition of belonging to the Moral Majority.

Despite gestures like these, Falwell never became popular with the Jewish community. Neither did Robertson, who received virtually no Jewish support when he ran for the GOP presidential nomination in 1988. Abortion was a major issue, and "choice" had overwhelming support among Jewish voters. "It is a mystery to me," he said, "how a people who toast *l'chaim*, to life, can champion killing babies."

Robertson also had a problem with the way secular Hollywood portrayed Christianity. In 1988, when Universal Studios produced *The Last Temptation of Christ*, a movie that portrayed Jesus as married to Mary Magdalene and engaging in sexual fantasies about the sisters of Lazarus while he was being crucified, Robertson appealed to Abe Foxman of the ADL to denounce the film and demonstrate that the Jewish leadership of America was concerned with the feelings of their Christian fellow citizens. Foxman replied that the American Jewish leadership did not, contrary to stereotypes, control the film industry.

Things got worse. In November 1989, Robertson went on his *700 Club* and warned that Jewish opposition to Christian symbols and customs could lead to a serious anti-Jewish backlash. He noted that the founder and current head of the studio that produced *The Last Temptation of Christ*, were Jews, as were all the controlling principals of the company. In the same screed, Robertson cited Jewish complaints about a Polish Carmelite convent located next to Auschwitz that had built a twenty-three-foot cross near the camp's gate. He accused "a strident minority within a minority of only five million" of undertaking the "systematic vilification, weakening and ultimate suppression of the majority point of view from society." He mentioned a private meeting, held a few weeks earlier in Atlanta by "the leaders of some of America's largest evangelical ministries" to take action to protect the rights and sensibilities of evangelicals and Roman Catholics against the onslaught of Jewish cultural and religious hostility.

For a decade, Eckstein had advocated for Robertson as a philo-Semite and a reliable friend of Israel. It was a reciprocal relationship; Robertson, perhaps more than any other Christian leader, had been responsible for helping the Fellowship get off the ground. But in mid-January 1990, Eckstein sent Robertson a letter calling his comments "blatantly skewed and objectionable." He reminded Robertson that his concern for the feelings of Roman Catholics, while touching, was not exactly consistent with the belief of many evangelicals that Roman Catholics are not Christian. (Robertson himself excluded Catholics from the faculty of his Regent University.) He also wondered why Robertson hadn't mentioned that the film's writer (Paul Schrader) and director (Martin Scorsese) were not Jews. "I wish to caution a sincere and sensitive Christian, whom I regard as a friend— both to me and this ministry—stay clear of Jew baiting and even the appearance of it," Eckstein wrote. "As tolerant as our society thankfully is, I do not believe we are immune from being provoked to hostility toward one another."

After this exchange, there was what Eckstein recalls as a "tepid" period in the relationship. But there was no break, as there had been with Dobson, and by 1994, Robertson (and Falwell) joined Eckstein in Chicago for a Fellowship event. The following year Robertson warmly endorsed Eckstein's new radio show, *Ask the Rabbi*. "This is a man of great integrity," he said. "I've known him for many years and I've seen a steadfast purpose to bring about a fellowship between Christians and Jews. I find him a man who is very strong in his own belief and has a warm heart for Christians as well as Jews. And I think he moves easily between both communities. He has been a stalwart witness for unity and love and I applaud what he does."

Unity wasn't in the cards, though. That year the ADL published a booklet, *The Religious Right: The Assault on Tolerance and Pluralism in America*, that accused the Christian Right of spreading hate and fear. They were "prophets of rage" whose goal was to build a Christian America in which there would be no place for Jews or other nonbelievers. Robertson, Falwell, and the others were depicted as enemies of civil liberties and the US Constitution. Evangelicals, infuriated, accused Foxman and his allies of slandering them to help the Democratic Party and to deny them their right to participate in the American cultural debate. They wondered at the perversity of Jewish leaders slandering their most reliable Christian allies.

Eckstein found himself in the middle of this fight, the one man able to communicate with both sides. With the blessings of both, and with the help of US Senate chaplain Lloyd Ogilvie, he sent out invitations to some twenty leaders to meet in the Senate building for a daylong, off-the-record forum. Falwell was present. Ralph Reed of the Christian Coalition represented Robertson. Foxman came too. So did the heads of Jewish and Christian denominations. The Jews sat on one side of a large, square table; the Christians on the other. At first the discussion was polite and cautious. But during a break, Ralph Reed crossed paths with Foxman and said, "How dare you call us anti-Semites." Foxman denied that he had ever used the term to describe evangelicals. Reed coldly stared at him and said, "You did call us anti-Semites."

At the conference table, the evangelicals, led by Reed, objected to direct-mail solicitations, sent by the ADL and other Jewish groups, which depicted the Religious Right as a menace to American democracy. "Foxman and the others were on the defensive," says Eckstein. "It was there, at the Senate building, that the ADL report on Christian extremism died." Jewish leaders agreed to stop sending out inflammatory fund-raising letters. Foxman declined to issue a formal apology, but he invited Reed to address an ADL meeting (and the AIPAC issued a similar invitation). The meeting was a watershed in the relations between two previously bitter enemies. It also marked the moment that Eckstein became smitten with Washington, DC. He had gathered people together to pursue his vision, and at the same time had learned how political influence is leveraged. "All that power, the sense that was I actualizing my spiritual calling through politics and that I was part of history, was heady. I was *seduced* by Washington."

Eight

❖

POTOMAC FEVER

In 1995, Eckstein founded the Center for Jewish and Christian Values, the Fellowship's Washington, DC, office, on Massachusetts Avenue. He imagined it as a bipartisan agency that would deal with a wide spectrum of religious issues, in the United States and internationally. His mission statement was simple and grandiose: "To bring disparate and polarized groups together to find common ground on issues of public concern." In other words, to create a Jewish-Christian lobby.

Back in Chicago, in his ADL days, Eckstein had started dealing with international human rights issues from an ecumenical and bipartisan perspective. He founded the Emergency Task Force for Indochinese Refugees (ETFIR), a lobby group that worked to help Vietnamese boat people enter the United States. The experience broadened his perspective. When a prominent apologist for the new regime in Hanoi came to town, a protest turned violent. Eckstein moved among the protesters trying to restore order. "One of them turned to me and said, 'Rabbi, you wouldn't be trying to calm things down if it was Hitler who was staying in this hotel.' The Hitler comparison went too far, but I understood what he was saying. It was easy for me to have perspective. For him, this wasn't just a question of international justice, it was personal. That has stayed with me and in some ways it complicates my life. I find it difficult not to see others' point of view."

Eckstein was also a founder of the American Refugee Committee, a Chicago-based group that worked to aid survivors of the Cambodian killing fields. In groups like these, Eckstein rubbed shoulders with national figures like former (and future) Defense Secretary Donald Rumsfeld and First Lady Rosalynn Carter. It gave him a taste for bigger things, and eventually led to the formation of his Center for Jewish and Christian Values. There he partnered with some of the country's leading legislators. Bob Asher, the Chicago businessman who had been an early supporter of the Fellowship, was close to Indiana Republican senator Dan Coats. An evangelical Christian, Coats agreed to serve as co-chairman of the new organization. Eckstein balanced him with a Jewish, Democratic senator, Joe Lieberman of Connecticut, who unlike most liberal Jewish lawmakers, was Orthodox and happy to build bridges to the Religious Right.

Eckstein sought to bring the same ecumenical bipartisanship in putting together his board of directors, but it wasn't easy. Most of the recruits were political and social conservatives: former Reagan UN ambassador Jeane Kirkpatrick; ex-Secretary of Education Bill Bennett;

Republican intellectual and activist William Kristol; Kansas senator Sam Brownback, a recent convert to Catholicism; diplomat and political scientist Elliott Abrams; and Christian political organizer Ralph Reed. Liberals were represented by Rabbi Yitz Greenberg, Eckstein's former teacher at Yeshiva University, and Rabbi David Saperstein, a progressive who led the Reform movement's social-action center in Washington. Eckstein hired Chris Gersten, a mid-level official in the first Bush administration, to run the Center's daily operations.

At the Center's opening session Eckstein spoke about his goals in terms of shared values—the same inclusive ideals he promoted when he encouraged evangelicals to describe America as "Judeo-Christian," rather than merely "Christian." His agenda sought the middle ground on social issues: encourage adoption, fight against gratuitous sex and violence in the entertainment business, and restore a sense of moral purpose to public education.

These were fine phrases, but in practice they proved very difficult to reconcile. The most contentious issue was the poisonous debate between supporters of "choice" and "life." Personally, Eckstein opposed elective abortion, but accepted the Talmudic principle that it is acceptable if it preserves the life of the mother—a position to the right of progressive activists like Saperstein but to the left of those evangelicals who regard it as infanticide. "My feeling was the same as President Clinton's and Hillary's," says Eckstein. "I thought we should accept *Roe v. Wade* but work through education to make abortion rare." He supported initiatives to allow moments of silence in schools in lieu of prayer. He also did what he could to influence Hollywood and television, particularly on their almost uniformly negative portrayals of evangelical Christians. "Show business was identified in *everyone's* mind as a Jewish business," he says.

The Center gave Eckstein a DC base, and he decided to concentrate his activities on the Senate, where Coats, Lieberman, and Chaplain Ogilvie could pave the way for him. He came to Washington at least once a week, crowding an already hectic schedule, and met with senators and congress members. On the day before Passover, he conducted a model Seder for several dozen senators and their aides; Joe Lieberman's daughter, the youngest person there, recited the ritual Four Questions. Eckstein commemorated the Center's first anniversary with a convention that drew more than fifty lawmakers. "I was so taken with the buzz, by the fact that famous and powerful people were calling me by my first name, and journalists sought me out for interviews. I remember thinking, Wow, I'm really in the big leagues now," he says. He began asking himself the question that often occurs to ambitious men when they arrive in Washington: "Why not me?"

Eckstein learned that Senator Paul Simon, a Democrat from Illinois, was planning to retire, and he began seriously considering a run for his seat. He discussed the idea with several of his Washington advisers and a few potential fund-raisers. The money would be there. He was an attractive and well-connected Chicagoan, a moderate Democrat built for the Clinton era. "I loved the idea of an Orthodox rabbi serving in the Senate, showing the world what our values are, *witnessing*," he says. "And, to be honest, it was an ego trip."

Despite his frenetic pace, Eckstein continued serving as the weekend rabbi in Evanston, and in August 1996, he delivered a political sermon to his congregation. The Republican convention had just nominated his friend Jack Kemp for the vice presidency. Kemp was a member of the Center's board of directors, and a voice for wholesome values. Eckstein called the congregation's attention to a poll that found "the primary concern of over 80 percent of Americans is not the economy but the moral condition of our nation. . . . Clearly Americans are deeply troubled by the deterioration of the moral fabric of our nation—the violence not only on TV and the media, but in our streets.

"It is for these reasons that, as many of you know, I founded the Center for Jewish and Christian Values," he said. "I believe our American society is rooted in an ethical value system based on our Torah and what Christians call the Old Testament. And while Jews and Christians differ often in matters of interpretation and application of these core values, I believe there is something called a Judeo-Christian heritage, a common value system and ethical agenda nurtured in and by our shared literature and religious heritage and serving as the foundations and pillars of American society. . . . Until the day we make aliyah and contribute to the moral fabric of Israeli life and society, we have a religious as well as a civic obligation here in America to rebuild the moral foundation of society using our Jewish tradition," he said. "Many of you will be surprised to learn that I am a Democrat who favors Clinton—but on whatever ticket we are with we are called to bring God's presence not only to the Jewish people but to the world."

Eckstein launched a few trial balloons, but there was no reaction in the Chicago media, and no evident enthusiasm in party circles. The Illinois Democrats already had a candidate, Dick Durbin. Eckstein dropped the idea of running for office, but he still wanted to be a player in Washington. He was attracted to the questions of freedom of religion, especially for Christians in nations where they were being persecuted. He began thinking about a project, and asked his friend, activist rabbi Yitz Greenberg, to come to Washington and explain to evangelical leaders how the international Jewish campaign to free Soviet Jewry had been organized. Eckstein also began working on freedom-of-worship problems in Muslim Africa, but the issue didn't really excite him (or anyone else). Then, during a Shabbat walk, an idea came to him.

He had read about a Christian pastor in China, Peter Xu Yongze, who had been sentenced to a long prison term for unsanctioned religious activity. A campaign to free him was getting under way, and Eckstein wanted to get involved. He went to the White House and met with an aide to President Clinton, who told him that, while the White House couldn't officially sponsor his mission, it would help him contact the government in Beijing.

In Beijing, Eckstein went to see Xe Sha Xan, the minister of religious affairs, and raised the issue of the imprisoned pastor. He also made contact with the so-called underground church—Christian congregations not sanctioned by the state. Eckstein was aware that he was being followed throughout his visit, and was careful to make contact with Christians from public pay phones. The mild cloak-and-dagger aspect appealed to him. "It wasn't really dangerous, as it would have been in the USSR at the time," he says. "But it would have been awkward if I had been caught."

During this and a subsequent visit, Eckstein was given official guest treatment, which included vegetarian feasts thrown by the minister of religion. "That was the first time I had been treated in that way, as someone special," he says. On Christmas Eve, Eckstein arranged to attend services at a party-approved Christian church, and he mentioned it to the minister, who surprised him by saying that his own son would be attending that night. "I was amazed by the power of God and the possibilities for change. Here was the Communist minister, an atheist, a member of a party that was denying religious freedom to hundreds of millions of people, and his own son was attending a church service on Christmas."

Eckstein hoped that he might be able to parlay his good relations with the minister into a prison meeting with Christian dissidents, but he was turned down. "They didn't have enough confidence in me to show me their prisons. I was disappointed, but there was no way I could launch a protest," he says. He was also attacked by some Western human rights advocates as a pawn of the Chinese government's effort to legitimize its treatment of Christians. In the end, Pastor Xu's prison term was reduced by more than half. "I don't know that my visit had anything to do with that, but at least they were aware that someone from outside was watching, that there were people with connections and influence who were interested in the case," he says. He returned to Washington and submitted a written report to Congress. It had been an interesting and rewarding experience, but it was clear to him that his future was not going to be in freelance international diplomacy. "I was dreaming of a Jesse Jackson thing, where I parachute in and get somebody freed. But this began to seem more like a 'Jackson to Eckstein' fantasy. I still believed deeply in the mission, but I realized that this was a long-term commitment needing singular focus and I wasn't prepared to dedicate my life to it. I felt my calling was to my own people." There were still impoverished Jews in the former Soviet Union, in Ethiopia, and in Israel itself. Helping them had always been a goal. Now it was to become an obsession.

Nine

❖

ISAIAH 58

Throughout the 1990s, immigrants from the former Soviet Union flooded into Israel, and contributions to the Wings of Eagles program grew apace. In 1992, the year the first telethon aired, the Fellowship took in $717,000 in contributions; five years later, it had grown to more than $12 million. By 2000, it reached almost $30 million.

When Eckstein started out, he had been an advocate for Israel and a teacher of Judaism to evangelicals. Now he sat at the controls of unanticipated wealth. Soviet immigration was sufficiently funded. What would he do with the extra money? The answer came to him in Chicago, while he was leading Yom Kippur prayers at the Park synagogue. The service includes God's rhetorical question to the Jews in the book of Isaiah: "Ye fast not this day so as to make your voice be heard on high. Is such the fast that I have chosen?" God provides his own answer with another question: "Is it not to give your bread to the hungry, and bring the poor that are cast out to your house, and when you see the naked, cover him?" Eckstein had read this passage every year of his adult life, but this time it struck a chord. "I realized that there were a lot of elderly Jews who wouldn't be able or willing to leave for Israel," he says. "It was pretty simple. They needed help, but there was no one taking care of them."

When Eckstein took the idea to his board of directors, he ran into stiff opposition. Evangelicals had given gladly to On Wings of Eagles, because they thought they were participating in a fulfillment of prophecy, the ingathering of the exiles. But helping impoverished Jews in Russia was a welfare program. There were poor people everywhere, and there were already Jewish welfare agencies, like the American Jewish Joint Distribution Committee. Eckstein insisted, and reluctantly, the board gave him permission to try.

The program needed a name that would resonate with evangelical donors, and so Eckstein chose "Isaiah 58," the prophetic chapter that had inspired him. He also needed an attractive appeal. The Fellowship had taken in most of its money on the strength of the initial telethon, *While the Door Is Still Open*. But that had starred Boone, Falwell, Robertson, and Hayford—four superstars of evangelical fund-raising. A subsequent effort, with Eckstein in the main role, had done comparatively poorly. He had natural gifts, but he needed a director who could teach him how to use them.

Lynn Doerschuk was a devout Christian who studied film at USC and specialized in religious fund-raising. Over the years he did specials starring Johnny Cash, Andy Griffith, Barbara Mandrell, and

Charlton Heston, and he had helped Dr. Stanley Mooneyham turn World Vision, an NGO that aids poor children, into a multimillion-dollar international agency. A mutual friend suggested that he get in touch with Eckstein, who was looking for someone who could help him make effective infomercials.

Doerschuk flew to Chicago and met Eckstein at a restaurant near O'Hare Airport. Doerschuk arrived first, and he was taken aback when Eckstein appeared. "This big guy walked in wearing jeans and a baseball cap. I took one look at him and thought, This is going to be one wasted trip."

Eckstein explained what the IFCJ was trying to accomplish in the area of Christian-Jewish fellowship. Doerschuk didn't have any idea what he was talking about. But when the conversation turned to fund-raising, the two began speaking a common language. Eckstein confessed that he had no idea how to replicate the success of the Boone show, and he wondered where he could find another evangel-ical showbiz figure.

Doerschuk said that wasn't necessary. His experience told him that often audiences regarded celebrity spokesmen as hired guns. Boone was different—his evangelical credentials and sincerity were widely acknowledged—but there were very few comparable stars. "What you need to do is find someone in the organization who is passionate and committed, and who can establish an immediate rapport with the audience," he said. That someone would be Yechiel.

They decided to do a trial run, a trip to Ukraine to visit elderly

Holocaust survivors in need of help. Doerschuk's plan was to shoot the infomercial like a news documentary, using a small crew and playing things by ear. He explained to Eckstein that they would be dealing with poor, simple people who would be intimidated by a major production. He wanted to keep the dynamic real.

Eckstein was skeptical. He had done scripted TV spots from Israel, and they had gone well. Though Doerschuk thought he could do better just winging it, Eckstein thought he needed a carefully vetted plan. He called Doerschuk nearly every day, asking to see the script. "I was worried about how I would come off. And it seemed to me that it was just filming without a plan or a structure. That made me very nervous." Doerschuk told him to relax; they would shoot their infomercial "run-and-gun" style.

They flew to Kiev, rented an SUV, and set out for what had once been the Jewish Pale of Settlement. As they drove out into the countryside, Eckstein peppered Doerschuk with concerns. Before World War II, the countryside had been dotted with Jewish villages, but the Nazis had wiped out most of the Jewish population, and the Communists had repressed the Judaism of the survivors. Few who remained spoke Yiddish (which Eckstein spoke with reasonable fluency) and virtually none knew English. Eckstein was afraid he wouldn't be able to communicate with them, or draw them out enough that they'd be vivid to his audience. He also worried that without a script he would freeze in front of the camera. It made for a tense ride.

Finally, the two men reached the town of Zhitomir, where they checked into a cavernous, empty hotel with bad food, worse plumbing, and no electricity. The hotel did have its own amenities, though. "When I got to the room, the phone rang. It was a hooker in the lobby, asking if I wanted some company. I laughed and told her no thanks. I am human, but I'm a rabbi. Besides, I thought it might be a setup by the KGB."

The next day they traveled to a Fellowship food-distribution center, in the ruins of an old synagogue. A small crowd had gathered. Eckstein once again asked for a script. Doerschuk told him to walk over to the crowd, greet them in the best way he could, turn to the camera, and explain where he was and what he was doing. The first takes went badly, with Eckstein camera-shy and stiff. Doerschuk prodded him. "I told him to just be yourself and express your passion," he recalls. "Tell the viewers why all this is going on."

Eckstein followed instructions. He found that he could tell the audience what he was doing, but he was unable to actually make a pitch for money. (When the film was completed, the "ask" was handled by an offscreen announcer.) His meetings with the Jews were emotional; in some of the televised scenes, tears rolled down his face. His Jewish critics might charge that it was staged, but they were mistaken. "I allowed myself to be vulnerable and it was my natural response," he says.

Even as Eckstein gradually assented to Doerschuk's direction, he repeatedly wondered aloud how the hours of film they were collecting could possibly be made into something coherent. Doerschuk just as repeatedly assured him that it would be fine. "I've worked with great actors on Christian fund-raising," says Doerschuk. "But Yechiel—and Pat Robertson—are in a league of their own. They know the content of their message and they have a passion for it. That's more engaging and powerful than anything a celebrity can bring. Yechiel was reluctant to get too emotional on camera. I explained to him that the camera doesn't know any more than it sees. If you aren't showing it, it isn't on the screen. I learned that when he encounters people who are suffering, and I gave him enough time, his sincerity and passion come across."

Doerschuk took the footage back to Nashville and edited it into a thirty-minute infomercial. Then he flew to Chicago and screened it for Eckstein. They watched in silence. At the end, Eckstein had tears in his eyes. "That's the most moving thing I've ever seen," he said. "I couldn't believe it was me in it."

Isaiah 58 was a fund-raising hit, bringing in millions of dollars. It had taken Eckstein years to get beyond his origins as a side bet by Jewish Republicans, but he was now fully launched, and he had learned from experience. At the time, companies that engaged in religious fund-raising sold their clients on the idea that television was a money loser in the beginning that could gradually pay dividends by building an audience. "Yechiel understood something very basic that almost nobody else back then got," says Lynn Doerschuk. "He realized that the point of doing this sort of advertising isn't to build on future projections. It is to create actual income right now. The first donation might also be the last, and it was important to make sure that it wasn't only a loss leader. It made a profit."

———

Eckstein made sure that the Fellowship kept meticulous records and paid keen attention to individual supporters. The generally accepted principle of fund-raising in most organizations is that 90 percent of funds are contributed by the wealthiest 10 percent of contributors. Eckstein inverted the pyramid. By the time *Isaiah 58* went on the air, 98 percent of his donors were evangelical Christians of modest means, and the average gift was about $75. Eckstein saw these as "sacrificial givers," and kept a file of donors who gave up their birthday money, did without luxuries, or dedicated a portion of their Social Security check to helping poor Jews. The days were long past that he could write a personal letter to every donor, but he saw to it that someone on his growing staff did. If a natural disaster struck, Fellowship staffers downloaded files of donors in the affected area and called to let them know that the rabbi was aware of the situation and would try to help in whatever way he could. If donors wrote in with personal problems, Eckstein said prayers for them at the Wailing Wall in Jerusalem. These were ways of keeping up contributions, yes, but they were also reflections of Eckstein's gratitude and pastoral care for the donors, many of whom considered him to be their spiritual leader. He had, as he sometimes half-joked, more Gentile followers than any rabbi since Jesus. Eckstein saw his donors as a congregation, willing to support causes he championed. A good many of the checks that arrived were made out simply to "The Rabbi." The board of directors stopped trying to second-guess his intuitions and simply backed him up.

Some, like John French, a successful Christian businessman, became his disciples. French and Eckstein met at Jamie Buckingham's funeral. Although French is a Protestant, he was living on Cape Cod in a Benedictine community whose seventy sisters and thirty brothers have taken a vow of celibacy. French had a longtime interest in Christian Zionism; he visited the Fellowship headquarters in Chicago and was impressed by the modesty of its facilities. When Eckstein invited him to join the board of directors, he readily agreed.

"The Holy Spirit created the relationship between me and Yechiel," French says. "I found in him a childlike humility that is God's gift. It became clear to me that God had anointed his ministry." French eventually became co-chairman of the board, along with Bob Mazer, one of the owners of the Chicago White Sox. From the beginning he saw his task in biblical terms; he was to act as an Aaron or a Hur, the loyal lieutenants of Moses, "upholding Yechiel's spirit and supporting him in whatever way we can. . . . His personal agony has been extreme. He has been rejected wherever he turned." But, he adds, "in the Roman Catholic Church, when they investigate someone for sainthood, the first thing they ask is, Did this person inspire a lot of controversy? If so, it is a sign you are doing God's work and not Satan's."

Not even French sees Eckstein as immortal, but as chairman of the board he hasn't been troubled by issues of succession, and he has resisted suggestions that there should be a contingency plan. "Yechiel is anointed. When the time comes, God will raise someone up."

French found virtue even in Eckstein's sometimes domineering leadership style. "He's stubborn, and he has insisted over the years on having things his way. At board meetings, from time to time, I stand behind him and rub his neck and say, 'You are nothing but a stiff-necked Jew.' But that's one of his strengths." Eckstein was pleased with French's characterization. He was, indeed, stiff-necked when it came to his principles. And he was happy to see that his Christian followers felt comfortable enough to kid him about it.

Eckstein's reasons for starting Isaiah 58 went beyond his desire to help the Jews of Russia. The project would keep him in the evangelical public eye. It would broaden the rationale for donating to the Fellowship, from participating in history through aliyah to assuming a "brother's keeper" obligation toward impoverished Jews. And it would enable him to strike a strategic alliance with the mainstream American Jewish community, via one of its most prestigious organizations, the Joint Distribution Committee. "It became clear to me that Christians would respond generously to what they, and I, saw to be the biblical injunction 'Comfort ye, comfort ye my people.' I knew the money would be forthcoming but I needed a structure to give it away. The Joint had that."

The JDC, also known as the Joint, was founded in 1914 as a welfare agency for the world's poorest Jews. Throughout the pogroms and the devastation of World War I, it provided aid in Russia, Central and Eastern Europe, and the newly settled area of Palestine. After Hitler came to power, it removed German Jews to boarding schools in Palestine. During the Cold War, the JDC was active in trying to aid Jews behind the Iron Curtain, and helped impoverished communities in

Iran, Morocco, and other Islamic countries. Since the fall of the USSR, it had been dispensing aid to the poor and elderly—the same community the Fellowship had singled out under Isaiah 58.

The JDC was interested in Eckstein's activities, which were complementary. But its directors had concerns about him and his organization. He was still an outlier in the philanthropic Jewish community. The mainstream *Hadassah Magazine* refused to run Fellowship ads. The head of the Jewish Agency for Israel, Avraham Burg, declined to be photographed with him. Eckstein was invited to a JDC board meeting, and he was aware that he would be facing a skeptical audience. "He came to tell us that evangelical Christians were our friends and potential partners," says Alan Gill, the CEO of the Joint. "There was a lot of trepidation among the staff and the lay leadership. People didn't know what was behind it. Why was a rabbi doing this? A rabbi advocating for evangelicals was confusing."

Eckstein delivered a bravura performance, assuring the assembled members of the establishment that he and they were on the same side. "He challenged us at that meeting, as a major Jewish organization, to open a new chapter in our relations with the evangelical world," Gill says. "He was there, he said, to help us get past our fear of the unknown. His message was: Let me help you get in sync with today instead of yesterday. As he spoke, you could sense the room tip."

A partnership with the Fellowship was a radical change for the JDC, which partnered with governments but had never worked with a non-Jewish organization. The JDC did due diligence and the Fellowship came up clean. "People were impressed by Yechiel's work in the former Soviet Union," says Gill. "There was no glory there, just helping a lot of elderly people." The JDC decided to go ahead with a joint venture.

It was a big moment for Eckstein and the Fellowship—the first time a major American Jewish organization embraced his mission and offered him a leadership position, first on its board of directors and later on the executive board. Over time, Eckstein channeled more than $100 million of Fellowship donations to impoverished Jews in the former Soviet Union, the Balkans, and Ethiopia through the Joint Distribution Committee.

"In the matrix of Jewish life, Yechiel is absolutely central," says Gill. "To me, it's just stunning that these Christians care about needy Jews. He's the one who awakened that concern."

Among the neediest of the world's Jews were the Beta Israel of Ethiopia. For centuries they had lived in the hinterland of the land of Kush, maintaining their traditional identity as members of the lost biblical tribe of Dan. In nearly total isolation from the Jewish world and, for that matter, from modernity, these pious people, subsistence farmers and goatherders, never doubted they were Israelites lost in the wilderness.

Such an exotic tribe intrigued occasional Jewish travelers to the region, but their claims were not taken seriously. Beta Israel's scripture was written in the Geez language. They knew nothing of the Talmud, standard Jewish prayers, or anything that had happened to Jews elsewhere in the previous two millennia. Indeed, they didn't know, until the first travelers began showing up in the nineteenth century, that there *were* other Jews in the world. The Beta Israel circumcised their children, refrained from food forbidden by the Torah, and strictly observed Shabbat. Most of all, they had a very strong attachment to Jerusalem and a belief that one day a Messiah would come and return them from exile.

The Russian-Polish Jewish socialists who founded the State of Israel were desperate to build a population. They welcomed immigrants with strange customs from Yemen, Iraq, Morocco, the Caucasus Mountains, India, and Persia. David Ben-Gurion and his associates were not particularly interested in every last nuance of the Judaism of the immigrants (a large part of the Bulgarian immigration, for example, consisted of the Christian neighbors of Jews, desperate to escape Communism). Instead, the Israeli leadership categorized the immigrants by their practical value. The Ethiopians— residents of a distant and underdeveloped country—were seen as "bad material," not worth an effort. Besides, the rabbis had serious doubts about the authenticity of their claim of Jewishness, which, had it been confirmed, would have enabled them to immigrate to Israel under the Law of Return. There was also an undeniable element of racism in the political establishment's reluctance to even consider bringing this tribe of alien blacks to Israel.

In the 1960s, a few Beta Israelites received help from American and European Jews to come to Israel. Their presence forced the rabbinate to consider the question of their bona fides. Ovadia Yosef, the chief Sephardic rabbi of Israel, studied the case and determined that the Beta Israel were, in fact, a long-lost branch of the Jewish people. They could be considered eligible for citizenship under the Law of Return if they were willing to undergo a relatively simple conversion ceremony. Ashkenazi chief rabbi Shlomo Goren disagreed. In any case, it was a moot point. The masses of Beta Israel had no way to get to Israel without aid, and the Israeli government didn't want them.

In 1977, shortly after Menachem Begin became prime minister, a small group of young Beta Israel men gathered in front of his office in Jerusalem, carrying homemade signs that read "Let My People Go"—the slogan of the Free Soviet Jewry movement. Begin sent an aide to invite two of the young demonstrators to meet with him. In Begin's office, they were speechless at first; finally one of them blurted, "My brothers are dying in Ethiopia!" Certainly the Beta Israel were suffering extreme poverty, and like their non-Jewish countrymen, they were endangered by the often capriciously murderous Mengistu regime.

Begin rose from his seat, embraced the young man, and said, "I will save *our* brothers." He called the head of the Mossad and ordered a secret rescue operation. Dubbed Operation Moses, it took time and diplomacy, but by 1984, an airlift brought more than ten thousand white-robed, black-skinned African Jews, almost none of whom had ever before seen an airplane, to Israel. Eckstein watched their arrival on TV, from Chicago. Struggling to keep his new Fellowship alive, he had no money to contribute, no donors to tap, no practical way of helping the newcomers to settle in Israel. But the scenes of men and women kissing the ground at Ben Gurion Airport fired his

Zionist imagination and he was certain that evangelicals would respond the same way.

In 1991, Israel mounted a second airlift from Ethiopia, called Operation Solomon. This time Eckstein was ready, and he launched a fund-raising campaign to help the immigrants come back to Zion. His donors responded eagerly to this opportunity to be a part of history. Over the next two decades, they contributed more than $100 million for causes that benefited the African Jews. But Eckstein was eager to do more than simply funnel money into the immigration budget of the quasi-governmental Jewish Agency. Shortly after Operation Solomon, he learned that a community of some 2,500 Jews in Qwara, a distant rural region of Ethiopia, had been left behind—the result of an internecine rivalry. The Jewish community of the area was at odds and separated by geography: some lived at the top of a mountain, some at the bottom. Here, as elsewhere in Ethiopia, Israeli officials depended on local spiritual leaders to draw up the list of eligible immigrants. Unfortunately for the Jews at the top of the mountain, the task was assigned to a "down the mountain" *kes*, a spiritual leader, who figured that Israel would be better off without the "up the mountain" faction.

When the mistake was discovered, the airlift was over and the government of Israel was eager to move on. Eckstein became the advocate for the left-behind Jews, lobbying the Knesset, pushing a reluctant bureaucracy, and finally arranging and paying for their return to their ancient homeland.

The Qwara Jews weren't the only ones feeling passed over. There were also the Falash Mura, a community of Ethiopian Jews who, generations earlier, converted to Christianity to avoid discrimination. Those who descended from a Jewish maternal line were Jewish under rabbinical law. Others, who had at least one Jewish grandparent, were eligible under Israel's Law of Return.

As the Ethiopian Jews left their transit camps in Addis Ababa and Gondar province, Falash Mura took their place and began agitating for an airlift of their own. The Israeli government was reluctant to mount a third operation, which would be both costly and complicated; among the Ethiopians now in the camps were many who had no claim whatever to Jewish ancestry and simply wanted a free ride to a developed nation. They would have to be individually examined by clerks from the Ministry of the Interior, the government said, and there was no budget for that. Eckstein called the government's bluff by offering to pay whatever it cost. "I had no idea how much that would be," he says, "but it was the right thing to do and I was confident I could raise the money." He flew to Ethiopia with a camera crew and was shocked by what he found.

"The camps were in horrible shape. People lived in appalling conditions," he recalls. "There was no electricity or running water. The kids were undernourished. They reminded me of the footage of the children in Biafra in the sixties. At first, I had a fear of even touching them. They were filthy, repulsive. There were open sewers in the camps, and I was constantly worried I would lose my footing and fall in. But I knew I couldn't help these Jews if I couldn't embrace them, not just figuratively but literally, and communicate with them in their own language. So I tried and I learned. I'd sit on the rock floor of their huts and drink *buna*, their version of coffee, and eat *injera*, a kind of bread made from rough flour, and talk to them, simple Amharic words they taught me. Eventually I became more comfortable and more knowledgeable. I was there to help and I needed to know how. Take food, for example. You have to feed people what they want to eat. You don't just order them pizza. I wanted them to choose what we brought them. It would give them a sense of independence, to empower them and to allow them to enjoy their meals." This seems obvious, but it is not. Foreign aid workers often try to forcibly improve the diets of the people they are feeding. He also brokered and funded an arrangement that brought Falash Mura to Israel in small groups over the next decade. When the last group arrived, in 2013, Eckstein was there at the airport in Tel Aviv to greet them in Amharic. With that, two thousand years of exile ended and the Ethiopian chapter of the return was completed.

Ten

❖

GUARDIAN OF ISRAEL

Once, in the early days of the Fellowship, Eckstein came to a meeting with Jerry Rose carrying a to-do list of fifty items—things like "start a public-service radio program," "have a conference in Washington, DC, on the differences and similarities between Jews and Christians," "inaugurate a Christian prayer service to commemorate the Holocaust," "reach out to the Hispanic community." Rose told him to cut the list down to four or five. Eckstein tried, but he has never mastered the art of condensation, or stopped coming up with new ideas, revised plans, and fresh challenges. What he did do was buy a small tape recorder that enables him to dictate a stream of reminders to himself and instructions to his staff. He's been using the same machine for thirty years, and he never goes anywhere without it.

At the end of 1983, as the Fellowship entered its second year, Eckstein told a reporter from the *Chicago Tribune* that he was pleased by the way things were going but that he "prayed for the day when I will be freed from all the fund-raising and office work and I am able just to pursue the vision." Thirty years later he was still praying for it. The search for the perfect management team has been an extended safari into the wilderness of frustration. Eckstein has hired a long line of men and women he was certain could step in and take over the administration of the Fellowship, and he has fired or driven away just about all of them.

"I admit that I am hard to work for, but that's mostly because I know everybody's job better than they do. I've licked stamps. I've sorted mail by zip code. I've carried things to the post office. I've spent days waiting by the mailbox, hoping a hundred-dollar check would come in and keep us going. I understand every part of what we are doing all over the world, and it frustrates me when others just don't do things the right way, or pay attention to detail. People say that I micromanage. Maybe so, but it doesn't seem that way to me. I kick the tires. I *check*. It's my Talmudic training. If you tell me a number, I remember it, and I expect it to be the same number next time you tell it to me."

The only senior staffer who has managed to stay with the Fellowship for more than a few years is executive vice president George Mamo, a soft-spoken and capable Baptist deacon with experience working for Feed the Children and other charities. Every member of Eckstein's senior staff has a story or two about a Yechiel explosion. One memorable eruption came during the summer of 2013, when he contracted to distribute ten thousand copies a day of an Israeli newspaper to old-age homes. The papers were supposed to arrive with his group's logo, but some didn't, and word reached Eckstein. He called the executive in charge and began the interrogation. *"How many were delivered? No, how many! Obviously you don't understand what I am asking. How many yesterday? Yesterday! How are you following up? Which homes received papers? No, precisely which ones? At what time of day? Morning newspapers aren't worth reading if they arrive in the afternoon! What do you mean you don't know what time? How could you not know what time? You are in charge of this. What, our logo wasn't on the paper? How many didn't? How could that be? Our donors are paying for this and they deserve the credit—humble Christians who are giving sacrificial amounts out of limited income! How are you fixing this? When will it be fixed? Next week? What day next week?"* When Eckstein got off the phone he was shaking with anger. But after a few minutes he calmed down and became contrite.

"I can turn into a monster," he says. "I can be a very bad manager. When I get upset by incompetence or lack of attention to detail. I intimidate people. I know I've alienated and mistreated a lot of staff over the years. I always apologize, but that isn't enough. I hate myself afterward. I feel I'm turning into a bitter old man." As self-criticism goes, this was exaggerated, Eckstein isn't a monster, but he can be a demanding and difficult boss.

Even Eckstein's daughters are not immune. "When I started working at the Fellowship, and I saw him in action, I was shocked," says Talia, who is on the staff in Chicago. "He's like a different person, Rabbi Jekyll and Mr. Hyde. He is so laid-back and easy in his personal life, completely nonjudgmental. Then he comes to the office and he is so intense, so driven. When he speaks to me in his work voice, I get offended."

Eckstein's centralized, abrasive, and compulsively quotidian management style will never be studied at Harvard Business School, but it works for him. In 2006, the Fellowship took in almost $75 million (and, through the crash and the subsequent seven years of recession he didn't have a single down year). Millions of evangelicals consider him their personal rabbi. All this has happened despite his patent inability to really trust anyone to do things the right way—which is, perhaps, inseparable from his desire to find a way to do things better.

In 1999, Eckstein went to the State Department to attend the swearing-in of the first ambassador under the new International Religious Freedom Act. The law, aimed at protecting worshippers around the world from persecution, made fostering freedom of religion a foreign-policy goal of the United States. It also created an ambassador-at-large who would see to its implementation. The Clinton administration's choice was an evangelical Christian Zionist, Bob Seiple, a marine fighter pilot in the Vietnam War and former head of World Vision. The State Department had opposed the law; it wasn't interested in looking too closely at the religious-freedom policies of countries like Russia, China, and Saudi Arabia. Eckstein's Center had lobbied hard for the legislation, and he was thrilled by his success, but the ceremony was bittersweet. "I sat in that room in the

Department of State, looking at the oil portraits on the wall, and I felt a sense of awe. This was where American history was made and I had just played a small role by helping to put the issue of religious freedom on the American agenda. Here I was, an Orthodox rabbi, helping defend persecuted Christians. I felt I was doing something important and right, but it was the wrong thing for me at that time. My dream, ever since I can remember, was to live in Israel. I was forty-nine years old, and I said to myself, If not now, when? I love America. But it didn't really feel like home. Right there, in the Roosevelt Room, I decided that it was time for me to make aliyah."

It was a decision that he knew would end his marriage. For years, relations between Yechiel and Bonnie had been increasingly distant. Yechiel knew that Bonnie was not willing to move to Israel with him. His daughters were grown and living their own lives. He left home and took an apartment in the city. For moral support he turned to his younger brother Berl and to his best friend, Chicago businessman and philanthropist George Hanus. "They were the ones I could talk to, share my pain with," he says. "It would have been very hard for me to get through the divorce without their support."

The day after Eckstein decided to move to Jerusalem, he convened the staff of the Center and announced that he was closing it. Joe Lieberman, a close friend, expressed support for the decision; as an Orthodox Jew, he understood the pull of Jerusalem. Others were upset. Senator and Center co-chairman Sam Brownback argued that the closing would leave Washington without a place for religiously and politically polarized leaders to come together. Some people thought he should turn the operation over to someone else. Gersten volunteered to stay on and take care of daily operations. But Eckstein, who was the Center's sole funder, decided to shut the doors, effectively ending the Fellowship's role in national politics. In retrospect, he thinks it was a mistake. "I guess it was a control issue," he says.

At the very least, closing the Center would prevent him from having to delegate authority, something he was never that happy doing. In any case, the situation in Washington had changed since Eckstein came to town. Israeli prime minister Benjamin "Bibi" Netanyahu and opposition leader Ehud Barak were both avid supporters of the alliance Eckstein had crafted. Barak, nominally a socialist, was listed as a faculty member at Pat Robertson's Regent University. Netanyahu, who served diplomatic stints in Washington and at the UN when the Religious Right was coming together, was a friend of Jerry Falwell's.

In 1998, the Clinton administration had undertaken a peace initiative aimed at creating a Palestinian state. The terms were unacceptable to the Israeli government, and Netanyahu came to Washington anticipating trouble. The night before his scheduled meeting with Clinton, Falwell invited Netanyahu to dinner at the Mayflower Hotel, where an audience of some one thousand evangelicals had assembled. He and Netanyahu had cooked up the event to put pressure on the White House, and it worked. The Monica Lewinsky scandal was sapping the president's political strength; taking on Republican Christian Zionists seemed like too much. Clinton backed off, and the pressure Netanyahu feared never came.

The Mayflower rally surprised Eckstein, who had been neither consulted nor invited. Had he been, he would have advised against such an open challenge to Clinton. "I really didn't know much about realpolitik," he says, "but I didn't think anyone would dare do something like that." In any case, it seemed clear to Eckstein that Israel no longer needed him as a go-between with American Christian Zionists.

In 2000, Yechiel voted for George W. Bush. It was the first time in his life that he voted for a Republican, and he did it even though his friend Joe Lieberman was the Democratic vice presidential candidate. Gore had been a reliable friend of Israel since the start of his career; he ran in the Democratic presidential primaries in 1988 as the candidate most approved by the American Israel Public Affairs Committee (AIPAC). But Bush was a born-again, Bible-believing Christian, which made him seem like a *more* reliable friend of Israel. It was a shrewd assessment. Under Bush, pressure on Israel of the kind that had brought Falwell's troops to Washington was relaxed. This wasn't simply Bush's doing. At the end of his presidency, Clinton convened a summit meeting at Camp David between the new Israeli prime minister, Ehud Barak, and Yasser Arafat. Clinton unveiled an American peace plan calling for a division of the West Bank and the establishment of a Palestinian state. Barak, despite opposition in Israel, agreed. Arafat turned it down and scuttled the negotiations. It was a clarifying moment. The attacks of 9/11 provided another. Afterward, Palestinians danced in the streets of the West Bank and Gaza. In the United States, polls showed that Israel was now more popular than at any other time in its history. It would be a decade before an American government tried seriously to impose unwelcome territorial concessions on Israel.

Before setting out on aliyah, Eckstein finally got some of the recognition he had long sought from the American Jewish establishment. At the annual General Assembly of the United Jewish Communities he received an award for his work with evangelicals on behalf of Israel and Jewish philanthropies. The General Assembly—a gathering of the most influential members of the mainstream American Jewish world—was a big deal to him, but his pleasure was diluted when he learned that the award would be given in a small room during a side-session of the convention. Not only would he be denied his moment in front of the full gathering, but when he was given the plaque, Abe Foxman demonstratively walked out and publicly denounced Eckstein for giving Jews a bad name by begging from Gentiles.

On May 18, 2000, the board of directors of the International Fellowship of Christians and Jews met in Chicago and ratified a broad slate of changes. The first order of business was a treasurer's report by Jeffrey Royer, who indicated that the organization was in excellent financial shape. The problem was finding ways to spend the money. The board had long since established the principle that the organization would disperse all its funds annually, ending each year at zero. "The goal is to make sure that the donors' money is used, not stored in an endowment," Eckstein says. "We don't have a rainy day philosophy. Our method is based on the belief that God will provide, and for all these years, he has."

Still, God helps those who help themselves. Over the years, the Fellowship had raised funds for bridge building, aliyah to Israel, aid to the impoverished Jews in the former Soviet Union and in the Diaspora, and for religious freedom and pro-Israel advocacy in Washington, DC. Now things were changing. Eckstein informed the board that he would be closing down the Washington Center— the first of his major projects that he folded. Educational activities and ecumenical activities, the Fellowship's original concentrations, would continue. But the main focus would now be philanthropy. To move this forward, Eckstein announced the establishment of a new program, Guardians of Israel, which he saw as a large-scale welfare initiative for the poor of Israel.

Guardians, like all the Fellowship's programs, came into being because Eckstein wanted it. A few years earlier, the board had resisted the idea of Isaiah 58, arguing that evangelicals wouldn't be particularly interested in the care and feeding of elderly Jews in the former Soviet Union. Eckstein had argued otherwise, and had been proved right. Still, some members of the board wondered if the evangelical grass roots would really be prepared to donate to what was, after all, a relatively prosperous modern nation with its own system of social welfare. With so many impoverished populations in the Third World, many of them Christian, why would American evangelicals give money to Israelis?

Eckstein's answer was simple: Genesis 12:3. If the past seventeen years had demonstrated anything, it was the eagerness of evangelicals to "bless Israel" in return for God's blessing. Until the Fellowship came along, there had been no avenue for such gestures. Evangelicals were on the outside, looking in at the Jewish world. This estrangement prevented Christian believers from fulfilling what the Bible told them was God's will. They wanted a personal relationship with the Jewish people, and it had been Eckstein's genius to see that nothing was more personal than a personal check.

Eckstein had stood up for them against their secular enemies, offered them respect and love, and included them in the family of Abraham. If the Rabbi asked them to become Guardians of Israel, they would gladly sign up. And if the details were still vague, well, they trusted he would put their money to good use. For the evangelical members of the board, like Barbara and Robert Walker, it was a simple act of faith, which Eckstein understood. "They see me as a link to 'Jesus the Jew,'" he says. "Someone through whom they can bond with the people, the land, and the God of Israel and discover the Jewish roots of their Christianity." The Jewish board members had a more mundane view of their leader: they simply looked at his track record and figured he knew what he was doing.

The main office, it was decided, would remain in Chicago, but the Fellowship needed to establish a physical presence in Jerusalem. Eckstein had his eye on a space on Mount Zion, the site of the Last Supper and King David's Tomb—a prime parcel of ecumenical real estate if ever there was one. The Fellowship had arranged for a twenty-five-year lease there with an option to buy, but the deal was in jeopardy; the rabbi of the Diaspora Yeshiva, also located on Mount Zion, was using his political influence to block it. Eckstein warned the board members that they might need an alternative location and got approval to spend up to $800,000.

Eckstein also raised the issue of his living accommodations. He would be commuting back and forth to the United States, and Jerusalem hotels were expensive. Besides, he wanted a real home. Members of the board suggested the organization buy a place for his use, but he said no. He had bitter memories of his mother groveling for a carpet and new furniture. Of course, this was different; he wasn't just a rabbi for hire. It was he who had personally raised the Fellowship's money and handpicked the board members. Still, he wanted to ensure his independence and decided to use his per diem allowance to stay in hotels.

In 2001, Eckstein published *The Journey Home*, a novel built around a trip to the Holy Land that he and his friend Jamie Buckingham had planned but were never able to take. "The idea was that he and I would climb Mount Sinai together, he as a Christian and I as a Jew, receiving God's word separately but together, holding hands." The novel's main character is a journalist, a lapsed evangelical, who sets out to write about the Holy Land with Eckstein as his guide. The book begins with the reporter making snarky comments about Israel, about religion in general, and about Judaism in particular. Eckstein responds by gently rebutting his arguments and helping him see the essential mutuality of Judaism and Christianity, the virtuous necessity of the State of Israel, and the rightness of brotherhood. At the end of the book, the reporter goes back to America with a renewed Christian faith and a strong Zionist sympathy. The Eckstein character decides that he must stay in Israel to fulfill his own destiny.

The Journey Home is not exactly an enduring work of literature, but it presents a very good picture of Yechiel Eckstein's view of Israel in the year of his aliyah. The journalist is quick to point out Israel's stereotypical flaws, and Yechiel even quicker to put the most benevolent face on them. Early in their visit, the fictional Jamie remarks on the large number of armed soldiers on the streets. Yechiel beats back the veiled suggestion of militarism. "In Israel," he says, "the people are with the army, if only because the people *are* the army." They check into their hotel, and Jamie wants to get a drink. Yechiel explains that Israel doesn't have a bar scene. "You just don't have the same culture of people going to bars to drown their sorrows over a drink, or even coming together socially to have a martini with friends. Israelis are much more inclined to sit around over coffee and cake, or go out for an ice cream." When the friends happen upon two male soldiers with arms draped over one another's shoulders, Jamie sings, "Love is in the air."

"They're not necessarily gay, Jamie," says Yechiel. "Nonsexual physical contact between people of the same sex is quite common here . . . it may also be because these boys and girls enter the army and live in close quarters together for a few years. They are likely just close friends who put their lives on the line for each other every day and express their camaraderie physically as well as emotionally."

On a Sunday morning walk through downtown Jerusalem, they spot a group of boys with ponytails and earrings getting on a bus. "Just like King David envisioned it," Jamie cracks. Yechiel admits that yes, some young people have surrendered their Zionist idealism to the temptations of mall culture and MTV. Sometimes, he says, he even thinks that young Palestinians, "desperately seeking a homeland and motivated by a sense of purpose," are more idealistic and motivated than Israeli kids. Almost instantly, he corrects himself. "Was I speaking badly of my own brothers and sisters? These young Israeli men would soon be spending three years in the army, defending the land and people of Israel . . . I vowed never again to judge my people negatively, earrings or no earrings. Never!"

Eckstein had been to Israel dozens of times since his years at the yeshiva, but his view of the country hadn't really changed: he remained in awe of the place and of the people. The existence of Israel, particularly after the Holocaust, is an epic story of heroism; for a certain kind of Jew, it is natural to see the country's warts as beauty marks. Yechiel thought it was heaven on earth. "When I first arrived I got a note from an Israeli friend: 'Finally you have come home.' When I read it, I fell to my knees and wept, thanking God for allowing me the privilege of experiencing this moment," he says.

For many Jews, moving to Israel is an emotional experience, and Yechiel Eckstein is nothing if not emotional. But more was involved. His ancestors had lived in Jerusalem, under harsh conditions, and now he was returning, bringing with him the means to help other impoverished families. He was starting a new life, all alone for the first time since his college years. And, of course, this was Jerusalem, Zion, the pinnacle of his spiritual journey. "I felt I was fulfilling my destiny," he says.

Eckstein's dream of establishing a headquarters on Mount Zion did not come true— the head rabbi of the Diaspora Yeshiva succeeded in killing the deal. Instead, he established his Israeli office in downtown Jerusalem. The staff was small, headed by Dvora Ganani, a seasoned Israeli government bureaucrat with excellent contacts who ran daily activities with an assistant, a part-time photojournalist, and a few outside consultants.

Eckstein now had to figure out how to coordinate two separate operations. At the Fellowship's headquarters in Chicago, ensconced in a downtown skyscraper, a staff of eighty or so works the phones, develops programs, prepares educational material, plans events, and generally keeps things humming. George Mamo, the executive vice president, is responsible for handling the donations that come in at the rate of six thousand gifts a day.

To distribute these funds in Israel, Eckstein founded a nonprofit called Keren L'Yedidut (the Friendship Fund). If the name sounds generically benign, it isn't by accident. Eckstein decided that a name that explicitly included Christians could be a public relations problem in Israel. As it turned out, the Israeli public has fewer problems with "Christian" than it does with "Friendship Fund," which strikes local ears as a strange concept. Israel has a long tradition of gathering donations from Jews around the world, but the money is normally raised by community appeals and funneled to the government through the Jewish Agency. Israelis have been habituated to regard these contributions as a sort of guilt tax on Jewish Zionists who don't want to live in Israel. For them, it seems natural that the foreign money would be disbursed by the government—Israel has had a welfare state mentality from the very beginning—or pay for someone's name to be attached to the wing of a hospital or a university building. Considering the country's confiscatory tax rates and the other obligations that come with citizenship, such as mandatory military reserve duty until the age of fifty for men, very few Israelis developed the American habit of voluntary philanthropy.

When Eckstein arrived with his checkbook and the intention of expressing Christian solidarity through social welfare, the idea raised skeptical eyebrows. When it became evident that the checks would actually clear, politicians began to come to meet him. They discovered a big, openhearted guy who introduced himself as a rabbi but was slow to judge, and who said things like, "I just hope to use this money to help needy people," and, "My Christian donors give to bless the Jews because they believe it is God's will." In short, he looked to them like an all-American sucker.

At first, that assessment wasn't far off. Eckstein came with a high opinion of the leaders of the Jewish state—who were, after all, the elected leaders of the *Jewish* state. But it was pretty hard to ignore reality. The Israeli establishment seemed like a crime family. The president, Moshe Katsav, was sent to prison for rape and obstruction of justice. The minister of defense was convicted of sexual assault. The minister of finance got five years for stealing more than $600,000.

The minister of justice was found guilty of committing perjury. A long list of Knesset members were also convicted of various felonies. The miscreants came from parties of the left, right, and center, Jewish and Druze, secular and religious. But Shas, the Haredi-Sephardic party that claimed the mantle of defender of the poor, easily led the league in corruption. Three of its cabinet members (and four additional Knesset members) were brought down by felony convictions.

Eckstein got his schooling in the ways of Israeli government from masters. One was Bibi Netanyahu. Although Netanyahu was already a supporter of the Fellowship, Eckstein perceived him, and his family, with some awe. Bibi's brother Yoni Netanyahu was killed rescuing civilian hostages from a terrorist gang in Entebbe, Uganda, in 1976. In 1996, Bibi became Israel's youngest prime minister. When Eckstein moved to Israel, though, Bibi was out of office and heading the opposition Likud Party. The two men bonded over their mutual regard for American evangelical support, and their belief that more Jews should move to Israel. With that in mind, Netanyahu asked Eckstein to fund a new program, Nefesh B'Nefesh (Soul by Soul), aimed at encouraging mass immigration from the United States. Netanyahu asked for $2 million; Eckstein said $1 million on condition that Jewish groups match the amount. Netanyahu agreed. But after ten months, he was unable to come up with the money. He came to Chicago and asked Eckstein to donate the entire sum. Eckstein objected, but in a face-to-face meeting, Netanyahu convinced the Fellowship board to grant the money, meant to provide financial incentive grants to prospective immigrants, as well as funding transportation to Israel. Eckstein abstained. It was, he recalls, the first time his board went against his clearly expressed wishes.

On July 9, 2002, five hundred and twenty-nine American Jewish immigrants deplaned at Ben Gurion Airport. It was the biggest day in memory for American aliyah, and certainly the most dramatic. The welcoming ceremony at the hangar was decorated with Nefesh B'Nefesh banners. But, Eckstein says, "contrary to our agreement with Nefesh B'Nefesh that everything be co-branded, the Fellowship's identity was buried." When Eckstein discovered that this was done in response to concerns about Orthodox opposition to the Fellowship, he broke relations with the group. "It was a breach of trust," he says, still indignant. "They weren't willing to give credit to our Christian donors who helped them get the project, literally, off the ground."

It was a sign of difficulties to come in operating a Christian-funded philanthropy in Israel. When Eckstein first came to Jerusalem, he hired a social worker to show him around town. "One rainy winter day we visited an Arab family, and the kids didn't have shoes, just these flimsy plastic slippers," he recalls. "I asked the social worker if she could help, and she shrugged and said that she didn't get any funds from the government for this sort of thing. Sometimes she gave people money out of her own pocket." Eckstein—who sees Muslims as "our brothers, or at least our cousins"—was open to helping, but there were barriers. The heart of Guardians is its offer to allow evangelicals to bless the Jewish people and be blessed in return. Muslims, the vast majority of Israel's Arab population, are not especially popular with evangelicals (and vice versa). On the other side, the political leadership of the Israeli Arabs tends to sympathize with the version of history that sees Jews as usurpers and oppressors. They are happy to take government welfare but have little trust in foreigners, especially rabbis, dispensing free money.

Eckstein decided to try to give money away via existing social welfare programs. Why duplicate what was already being done? But when he tried to give Hadassah hospital a helicopter for emergency medical treatment, bureaucratic red tape over landing facilities ensured that the copter never got off the ground. He made a deal with one of the major bus companies to armor buses during a period of terror attacks, but the project got hung up in regulations and the need passed. He spent three fruitless years trying to get the government to partner with him on a national food security bank. Part of the problem was cultural. Eckstein spoke Hebrew, but he didn't really speak Israeli, and vice versa. Israelis tend to confuse good manners with agreement (this is an enduring problem of Israeli diplomacy, as well). Americans sometimes take hyper-confident assurances that everything is fine a bit too literally. But here, too, there were political problems. In the formative years of Keren, the Shas Party usually controlled the ministries that fund social welfare programs. The party's cabinet ministers, following the edict of their spiritual leader Rabbi Ovadia Yosef, worked to undermine Eckstein, effectively cutting him off from participating in public poverty programs.

Keren began donating to NGOs and funding only selected government initiatives. Eckstein handed out money to needy Boy and Girl Scout troops, built hospital trauma centers, and established dental clinics; he subsidized old-age homes and institutions for troubled children, opened soup kitchens, and put up homeless people in shelters. The idea was to help the helpless but there was no theme to the giving. Instead, Eckstein spun a web of freelance philanthropy based on little more than his optimism, his charitable instincts, and his good intentions.

Shortly after Eckstein arrived, he met with Prime Minister Ehud Barak and made a personal request: he wanted to serve in the army, to defend his new homeland alongside his earringed brothers. Barak, one of Israel's most decorated soldiers, turned him down. He appreciated the gesture, he explained, but the Israel Defense Forces (IDF) doesn't take volunteers on the cusp of fifty. He assured Eckstein that his civilian contribution would be more than sufficient. Eckstein knew that Barak was right, but he was dissatisfied. "I have never completely forgiven myself for my failure as a young man to respond to Moses's challenge, to join my brothers and assume my share of war's burdens," he says.

Eckstein found another way to contribute to the fight—one that did a great deal to establish him in Israel. A few months after he moved to Jerusalem, the Second Intifada broke out. It had been simmering since the 1995 Oslo Accords, in which Arafat agreed to recognize Israel in return for Palestinian autonomy in most of the

West Bank and Gaza. The deal was billed as a prelude to peace, but it didn't work out that way. Instead, Prime Minister Yitzhak Rabin was assassinated by a Jewish fanatic, who was furious at the terms of the deal. The Palestinians, for their part, sent terrorists to strike again and again. A Passover Seder was attacked, massacring tens of worshippers. Buses were blown up. Twenty-one kids were murdered on the Tel Aviv beach. Jerusalem was especially hard hit. Fifteen civilians, many of them teenagers, were blown up in a downtown pizza parlor. Hamas bombed a school bus, killing twenty-three. The capital became a ghost town after dark, with the few restaurants and theaters that stayed open at night obliged to bring in armed guards.

The intifada confronted Eckstein with both personal and professional challenges. For one thing, some evangelical donors were reluctant to support the Wings immigration program because they feared it was bringing Russian Jews into a war zone. Eckstein himself lived in a neighborhood that abutted several Palestinian villages, and like everyone else he was exposed to danger, at home and in the street. He especially worried about the safety of his daughter Yael, who was studying in Jerusalem at the time; she often took buses, which were a prime terrorist target, and she had a couple of close calls. Yechiel couldn't stop wondering how he would react in an emergency. Suppose he was downtown and came across a Palestinian mob attacking a Jew? Or, for that matter, a Jewish mob attacking a Palestinian? Would he have the courage and presence of mind to intervene? What would he do if a bomb left injured people lying in the streets? Would he stand frozen, as he had when he and Frankie Rosen discovered the body in the swimming pool in Ottawa? He began quietly practicing quick reactions, rushing to help elderly people who seemed unsteady on their feet and stopping at the scene of car accidents to offer help. "It's a Zen thing," he says. "My instinct isn't to be the one who jumps on the grenade. Heroic actions don't happen in a vacuum. They result from thousands of small acts." Would he jump on the grenade today? "I ask myself that often," he says. "I won't know until I'm tested. I hope so. But, to be honest, I hope I never am tested."

Professionally, he was more self-confident. Guardians of Israel, Eckstein's social welfare organization, added a new program to its roster, the Israeli Victims of Terror Fund. The original idea was to give grants to people injured in attacks or to their families, but the government of Israel took care of these expenses. So Eckstein used the funds to build or maintain physical and psychological trauma centers in hospitals throughout the country, and to underwrite ZAKA, a first-responder organization run by ultra-Orthodox volunteers.

He appealed for funds, and his donors responded. Income went from about $28 million in 2000 to $35 million in 2002, the first year the Terror Fund was in operation. Over the course of the Second Intifada, which ended in 2005, the Fellowship's annual donation grew to almost $50 million. "Anytime there is war or terrorism in Israel that's covered in the American media, it inspires those Christians who love Israel to help even more."

In addition to the money he raised, Eckstein appealed to evangelicals through direct mail and infomercials to travel to Israel as a show of solidarity. During the intifada, many American Jewish groups had canceled trips to Israel, leaving the hotels empty. Only evangelicals continued to arrive in large numbers. They saved the tourism industry, one of Israel's most important sources of foreign currency. Just as important, their presence made a lasting impression on the Israeli attitude toward Christian Zionists. In 2005, Eckstein inaugurated and led what became an annual Fellowship pilgrimage to the Holy Land.

Eleven

❖

ATTACK OF THE BLACK HATS

As a yeshiva student in Israel, Yechiel had been enchanted by the Haredim, God-fearers whose lives are ruled by rabbinical law. On visits to his extended family, he met their men with long beards and side curls dressed in black robes, and women in long, shapeless dresses, their hair covered with shawls or unfashionable wigs. Most spoke Yiddish; Hebrew, the holy language of the Torah, is frowned upon in mundane conversation. Children were everywhere, products of a literal reading of the biblical command "Be fruitful and multiply." Eckstein saw them as survivors, inspiring examples of what true Jews were supposed to be. As with many kids who had been raised in the modern Orthodox world, the compromises he had made with modernity left him feeling somehow less *Jewish* than these fundamentalist relatives, who seemed immune to the distractions of the twentieth century. One of Eckstein's heroes was Franz Rosenzweig, the secular

German Jewish philosopher who, when asked if he put on tefillin every morning, replied, "Not yet." The struggle to become ever more pious was, in Yechiel's mind, a climb up the scale of Jewish authenticity. He was not ready to trade in his baseball cap or knitted yarmulke for a black hat—or to segregate himself from the opposite sex, to live on alms as an impoverished student of the Talmud, or to remain in a self-imposed ghetto following the rulings of octogenarian rabbis. But he saw those who did as the truest keepers of the flame.

He was bothered, of course, by the fact that many Haredim, including some of his own family, were anti-Zionists who thought the State of Israel was a secular heresy. He was proud of one uncle, Lazar Dovid, who had bucked tradition and signed up for the Israeli army, and even lost a leg to a landmine. He never accepted the Haredi argument that studying Talmud was a greater mitzvah than self-defense, although he understood the original decision by David Ben-Gurion in the War of Independence to exempt a few hundred yeshiva boys on the grounds that Hitler had wiped out most of the Talmud scholars of Europe.

Eckstein had a special affection for the Hasidic branch of the Haredi world. Hasidism began as a mystical, charismatic, and highly emotional form of worship that swept the villages and ghettos of eastern Europe in the eighteenth century. The originator was Yisroel Ben Eliezer, known as Baal Shem Tov (Master of the Good Name). After his death, Hasidim splintered into sects led by venerated rabbis who were thought to have spiritual, even magical, powers. The Ecksteins of Jerusalem, through marriage, became aligned with a sect called the Karliners, for the town in Belarus where the dynasty began.

In his book, *The Journey Home*, Eckstein describes taking his Christian friend Jamie to the run-down Karliner shul in the ultra-Orthodox section of Jerusalem, Mea Shearim, where each Shabbat the men of the group share a meal with their rabbi. As Yechiel explains who they will be visiting, Jamie says that they sound reactionary and extreme. Yechiel protests, "They are actually very tolerant and loving toward me, in spite of our religious differences." The evening went well. Eckstein was warmly welcomed as family from America. (As for Jamie, Yechiel passed him off as a Jew; tolerance for Gentiles goes only so far.) On the walk home, Jamie was moved to recite the words of a psalm he had learned as a Baptist Sunday school boy: "How good and how pleasant it is for brethren to dwell together in unity."

But there is another Mea Shearim, one that Yechiel didn't share with his friend Jamie. Filmmaker Lynn Doerschuk saw it, though. Shooting a half-hour documentary in Mea Shearim, intended to help Christians understand Judaism, Doerschuk was taken aback by the animosity they encountered. "People would look at us, whisper, and literally cross over to the other side of the street—just scattering when they saw us." A local social worker Eckstein had hired as a guide said that word had spread that Eckstein took money from Christians. As they walked along, Doerschuk noticed posters of Eckstein's likeness with an X drawn through his face and a Hebrew phrase underneath. Eckstein translated it: "We will pursue you unto death."

Eckstein was able to ignore the threat, but he couldn't change the hostility. "The social worker took us to a family with a bunch of kids, all of them looking severely malnourished," recalls Doerschuk. "The father had nothing at all, but he absolutely refused to take money from us. Yechiel sent the social worker to buy them food, and he and Doerschuk left. When the social worker caught up to them later, he was carrying two large grocery bags. "They wouldn't take it because they know it comes from you," he told Eckstein.

Mea Shearim became an emblem of the opposition to Christian philanthropy. Unbeknownst to the black hats (and to Eckstein) the neighborhood had been planned in the nineteenth century by a German evangelical missionary, an architect named Conrad Schick. It was constructed for pious Jews by a European building society made up of an ecumenical collection of Jews and Christians—a precursor of Eckstein's Fellowship.

The idea that it was better to starve than to accept charity from Christians was not confined to the black hats. It found another champion in Mina Fenton, a member of the Jerusalem City Council. Fenton belonged to the National Religious Party, a modern Orthodox party that had been moving ideologically rightward for several decades. Known in political circles as a firebrand and an eccentric, Fenton played a role in blocking the Fellowship from getting office space on Mount Zion, and she whipped up opposition to Eckstein in rabbinical circles, charging that his self-description as a "bridge builder" was Christian code for "missionary."

Fenton's inspiration in this campaign was Rabbi Moshe Tendler, whose father-in-law, Rabbi Moshe Feinstein, had been one of the leaders of the anti-ecumenical movement in American Orthodoxy. Tendler was an esteemed Talmud scholar, an authority on Jewish law and medicine, and a member of the faculty of Yeshiva University. He had thought highly enough of Eckstein that his congregation in Monsey, New York, hired him, in his days as a YU student, to lead the youth group. Eckstein brought energy to the job, organizing bowling trips and song sessions, but Tendler didn't like it, especially because Eckstein allowed boys and girls to socialize. Years later, Tendler became a vocal opponent of the Fellowship, and on the eve of Eckstein's aliyah, he sent a warning to his colleagues in Israel. "Yechiel Eckstein has left Judaism and he must be excommunicated by the rabbis of the Land of Israel."

The rabbis were listening—at least the ultra-Orthodox ones were. In July 2001, the country's eighty-seven-year-old chief Ashkenazi rabbi, Avraham Shapira, published an official letter attacking Eckstein for spreading money that came from Christians, especially American Christians. "It must be realized that these monies are targeted to expand Christian missionary propaganda with the object of promulgating the religion of their 'messiah' and this is proven by their own publications," he wrote. "Therefore all who support them, whether it is accepting their monetary contributions or transfer of their financial support to institutions, are partners in strengthening the power of foreign idol worship in Israel, for which there is no atonement, and [will] lose both their worlds, this and the next." In other words, Jews who accepted money from Eckstein would be excommunicated now and go to hell later.

"We will neither remain quiet nor rest until this phenomenon of assisting or promoting such idol worship is consumed and erased from our midst," Shapira proclaimed. "Unfortunately, it is allowed to occur because of the ignorance of those in charge of our institutions and those honorable individuals whose eyes are blinded by the monetary contributions they receive. . . . Anyone assisting this in any way must be aware of his own trespass of a sin for which the principle of 'die rather than practice' is applied."

Shapira ended with a request to other rabbis, including those under his control—who are, in the Israeli system, civil servants—to spread the word and respect his boycott. The chief Sephardic rabbi, Mordechai Eliyahu, added his condemnation of Eckstein's operation. Eckstein was upset, but he saw the larger context. Chief rabbis in Israel are political figures, and both Shapira and Eliyahu were creatures of their parties. He was truly hurt, though, when the most prestigious Haredi Talmud scholar in Israel, Rabbi Yosef Shalom Eliashiv, signed a letter forbidding cooperation with Eckstein, calling it a "desecration of God." Eliashiv, past his hundredth birthday, was not at the height of his intellectual powers, but Eckstein badly wanted to meet with him and convince him that the Fellowship and its activities were good for the Jews. It was a discussion Eliashiv (or, more probably, the people around him) did not want to take place, and it didn't.

Other prominent black-hat rabbis aligned themselves against Eckstein. One of the most vociferous was Simcha Hacohen Kook, the chief rabbi of the city of Rehovot and a nephew of the venerated Rabbi Kook—the same Rabbi Kook who advised the young Yechiel Eckstein to disobey his parents and stay in Israel. Rabbi Shlomo Aviner, considered one of the more moderate spiritual leaders of religious

Zionism, ruled that it was forbidden for a dying patient to accept medication purchased by Eckstein's group, and if someone received it by mistake he must return it to "preserve the purity of his soul."

These opinions echoed across continents. In 2004, Tendler received a letter from "a loyal servant of God" inquiring whether it would be appropriate to invite Rabbi Eckstein to address his congregation in the United States. Tendler replied, "He is a danger to the souls of our brethren, especially those from the former Soviet Union who are unschooled in their knowledge of authentic Judaism. To offer Eckstein a stage to project his perverted sense of proper Jewish-Christian interactions would be a serious violation of Halacha."

Eckstein was confounded and angry; none of his rabbinical critics had bothered to meet with him, read his books, or take into account the good he was doing. "They were just giving in to political pressure," he says. "I told myself that these rabbis are not my rabbis, and there was no point in arguing. A friend advised me, 'Don't get into a pissing match with them,' and I didn't."

But Eckstein could not avoid the problem this rabbinical animosity posed for his philanthropic work. The ultra-Orthodox are Israel's poorest population. Their poverty is self-inflicted—they eschew birth control and have huge families; withhold secular education, which could allow their children to find jobs; and generally refuse to serve in the army. Roughly 40 percent of men are unemployed, and few women are permitted to work outside the home. But, like the father of the starving children in Mea Shearim who had rejected his groceries, they were prohibited from accepting his nonkosher Christian aid money. "I was always troubled by this: Why should children suffer because of the bigotry of their rabbis?" says Eckstein.

At some level, he knew that he had brought some of the disapprobation on himself. The rabbis may not have read his books, but they had heard a few suspicious-sounding excerpts. Toward the end of *The Journey Home*, for example, he and Jamie visit Jerusalem's Garden Tomb, which Protestants believe is the site of Calvary. The tomb inspires Eckstein to reflect that religion "is but the raft that enables us to cross the river of life and reach the other side. Judaism is my raft. Christianity is Jamie's. And we ought not to confuse the raft with the other side. We dare not absolutize the raft and imbue it with exclusive truth. To do so is idolatry, which, like Paul Tillich, I understand as misplaced ultimacy." In other words, Judaism is no better, no truer, and no more sacred, than Christianity or any other religion. To rabbis who consider other religions idol worship, these are fighting words. And invoking the authority of Paul Tillich, a Christian theologian, only compounds the crime.

There was more. Eckstein describes leaving the Garden Tomb where he passes a sign from Romans 1:4: "Jesus Christ was declared with power to be the Son of God by his resurrection from the dead." "A Jewish man passing by saw me coming out with my yarmulke," Eckstein writes, "and he turned away indignantly, no doubt assuming that I am a Jew for Jesus. While I still don't believe in Jesus as the

Christ, as Jamie does, and view him instead as a Jew who brought salvation to the Gentiles, in some respects that is exactly what I have become . . . a Jew for Jesus."

Why would Eckstein write such a thing? He had spent years trying to convince Jews in America and Israel that he was not a secret Christian or a missionary. He certainly knew that calling himself a "Jew for Jesus"—regardless of the context, the qualifiers, and the emphatic disclaimer—would be a provocation to the Rabbi Tendlers and Mina Fentons of the world. "I wanted to endear myself to Christian readers," he says. "But more than that, I wanted to tell the truth. It was the way I felt, not that I thought Jesus is the Messiah—I made that clear in the book. But I genuinely believe that Jesus was and is a force for good and for bringing salvation to Gentiles. It never occurred to me that people in Israel would take the statement out of context and use it against me." Still, in retrospect he regrets it. "If I could I'd probably delete that passage," he says, "not because I didn't believe what I wrote but because it wasn't worth the venomous attacks."

The Journey Home was self-published and came with a separate note of apology to the reader. "As you will notice, G-d's name was inadvertently used as a visual break between sections of text. That was an error that will not be repeated in the second edition. After consulting with the Chief Rabbi of Israel, Bakshi Doron, I received permission to distribute the remaining copies of this book since, unlike a newspaper or magazine which is treated lightly and thrown out, a book is not. Please, however, treat this book with deference and respect."

This was ironic: even as Eckstein bucked the rabbinical establishment, he felt the need for permission from a chief rabbi to distribute his "heretical" book.

Eckstein's fights with the rabbis have continued intermittently. One of the most prominent was with Meir Porush, a member of the Foreign Affairs and Security Committee of the Knesset and one of the stalwarts of the ultra-Orthodox Agudat Yisrael political party. In 2006, Porush came to Eckstein and asked for money to fund a seniors' home in the ultra-Orthodox town of Emmanuel. Eckstein agreed to donate $30,000. The grant immediately stirred opposition in black-hat circles. This was partly theological, partly political—Porush had rivals who didn't like seeing him portrayed as the savior of the old-age home. When the grant came to light, Porush issued a press statement admitting he had taken the money but claiming it was all a big mistake. "At the time we had no idea of the nature of the fund and since then we have had no connection with or correspondence with it," he told the press.

Eckstein had a similar experience with his friend Rabbi David Grossman, the founder and headmaster of a large orphanage and children's home in the Galilee town of Migdal Ha'Emek. With Eckstein's help, the institution flourished, and Grossman happily conducted tours for the Christian donors who came to see their money in action. But when he decided to run for chief rabbi of Jerusalem, he dropped Eckstein and publicly promised he would take no more tainted money. He even insisted that his image be removed from the Fellowship's television footage, which cost the group $25,000. "I was deeply hurt by this," says Eckstein. "Rabbi Grossman was a dear friend. He let his political ambitions get in the way of our friendship, and more importantly, of doing the right thing. So he caved in to political pressure, deprived his students of the help we were giving them. And he lost the election anyway."

After dropping his candidacy, Grossman sent emissaries to feel out Eckstein's willingness to restart the partnership. Eckstein agreed. "I pitied him," he says. Grossman, not surprisingly, asked for funds. Eckstein said he would consider it if Grossman would publicly give credit to the Fellowship. Grossman got the message and went looking for money elsewhere.

The cases of Grossman and Porush were hardly exceptional. Many of the most prominent political rabbis in Israel have denounced Eckstein in public while privately soliciting his help. Rabbi Ovadia Yosef, the former Sephardic chief rabbi and leader of the Shas Party, ruled unsparingly that Christian money was nonkosher—until his party was excluded from the governing coalition in 2012. That meant Shas lost access to public funds. Within days, Eckstein began receiving messages that the rabbi would be very pleased to welcome him for a visit. There was a time, early in Eckstein's years in Israel, when he would have responded to such an overture out of respect. That time is long past. He told a *Jerusalem Post* reporter that he would publish the names of the Haredi institutions that were taking money from him under the table. "I considered putting an ad in the paper with the list, but I decided not to. It would have been petty."

Three years after Rabbi Meir Porush's public denunciation of Christian money, he asked for another meeting with Eckstein. Porush

declined to come to the Fellowship office, so they met at a Jerusalem hotel. Porush began by briefing Eckstein on the situation in the
region, from the perspective of the Knesset Security and Defense
Committee. Eckstein, whose information on these topics is in no
way inferior to Porush's, listened politely. "Nobody comes to see me
unless they are going to ask for money," he says. "I try to make people not feel uncomfortable, so I listen to the preliminaries. I know
how difficult it is to ask."

Eventually Porush got to the point. He needed money for an Ashkenazi girls' school in Emmanuel, because the ultra-Orthodox parents,
his constituents, didn't want their daughters mixing with Sephardic
and Ethiopian students. Eckstein said, "Before you make a formal
request, check with the school to make sure it will take the funds from
us. I don't want to go through the entire bureaucratic process and find
out at the end that your rabbis there say it is forbidden."

Porush professed astonishment that Rabbi Eckstein could even
imagine such a thing might happen. Eckstein assured him that it had,
many times. "You were one of the people who rejected our funds," he
said mildly. "Not only that, you called us Christian missionaries."

Porush denied it. "I never said such things, but if you feel that I
have offended you in any way, then of course I apologize."

Eckstein went back to his office and instructed his staff to send
Rabbi Porush a copy of the newspaper article in which he had attacked
their work in Israel. Porush got the message: He and his fellow black
hats were free to despise Christian Zionists, but Eckstein wasn't
going to finance institutions that were built to perpetuate intolerance.

Twelve

❖

NEW BEGINNINGS

Yechiel Eckstein was finding his way in Israel, but there was something missing. His bicontinental existence and packed schedule never completely filled the void left by his broken marriage; he was a born family man without a family, and loneliness nagged at him. He met plenty of attractive women, but he was inexperienced and uninterested in dating; he wanted a wife, even if he didn't know how or where to find one. The woman of his dreams wasn't easy to come by. She had to be a Zionist willing to live in Jerusalem, a strictly observant Jew who would keep a kosher home and honor the Sabbath. She had to be open-minded enough to accept Eckstein's unorthodox mission and his evangelical friendships, sufficiently spiritual to understand his compulsive search for a connection with God, and independent enough to marry a man who never stayed still and had a million airline miles to prove it. He wanted a woman with a warm personality, able to soothe his emotional neediness. And he wanted someone he considered as beautiful and stylish as his mother.

Eckstein knew it was a big ask. On a trip to New York, he made a visit to the Ohel, the tomb of the Lubavitcher Rebbe in Queens, where he wept and asked God to send him a wife. He is not a big believer in "rebbe power," he says, but he was willing to try anything. "I felt like I was sinking into a dark, bottomless pit," he recalls. His doctor put him on an antidepressant, which helped, but it carried a professional price—it flattened his emotions and made him unable to shed tears of compassion, as he had in his infomercials. It also inhibited his praying. "I could no longer reach the same spiritual highs when I daven," he says. "I was willing to give up the extreme highs and lows for the sake of stability, but I can't lie, I missed the highs."

He found some solace in meditation. Ever since he encountered Buddhism as a student at Columbia and Union Theological Seminary, he has been drawn to Eastern spirituality. Now he began reading books by Eckhart Tolle (*The Power of Now*), Vietnamese Zen master Thich Nhat Hanh, New Age guru Deepak Chopra, and other Buddhist-influenced metaphysicians. During a trip he made to India to assess the needs of the Jewish community, he traveled by train from Mumbai to Dharamsala, a twenty-four-hour trip over rough tracks, to visit the Dalai Lama's palace, where he spent three days meditating with the monks. "One of the problems of depression is that you live in your mind too much," he says. "Meditating helps me realize I am alive, to connect my mind to my body." Connecting with himself was fine, of course, but it didn't really replace a connection with a partner.

In 2004, in the midst of a bout of the blues, Eckstein went to a business meeting in Jerusalem at Keren Hayesod, the public holding organization that handled Keren L'Yedidut's money. He was upset about various flaws in the organization's practices, and he let everyone in the room know it. One of them was a young woman named Joelle Medina. "He didn't know me, but I had seen him once before, at the first annual banquet of Keren L'Yedidut," she recalls. "He spoke that night and he was funny, self-confident, a *celebrity*. I thought, Wow! But it didn't really occur to me that I would ever meet him."

Joelle was dubious when her friend Dvora Ganani, Eckstein's director general, suggested fixing them up. "I hesitated because I was in awe of him. But I said yes." Yechiel called the next day. They spoke for an hour, and the next night they went out to a dairy restaurant. Joelle was born and raised in Barcelona, the daughter of a New York–born Sephardic Jewish mother and a Moroccan Jewish father. At fifteen, she had left home and moved to Israel; like Eckstein, she spent her adolescence living in a dormitory in a foreign country. She, too, was recently divorced, and she had two kids. As they chatted, he learned that Joelle spoke perfect English (and Spanish and French) as well as Hebrew—a big plus in Eckstein's world. She was happy living in Jerusalem. She and her first husband had owned a tourism business that specialized in evangelical Christian pilgrims, so she understood and sympathized with his mission. She was certainly religious enough for him. And she easily passed the "Belle Eckstein test." Sometime on that first date, a click was faintly heard.

Still, there was no rush to the altar. On their second date, Yechiel informed her that it was too early for him to get serious. The pain of his divorce was still too fresh and anyway, he was constantly on the road. Joelle was in no hurry either. She accepted his offer of friendship, and they got together whenever he was in town.

Joelle was astonished to find how unworldly Yechiel could be. He had been to dozens of countries, but had never been to the beach in Tel Aviv. He was a frequently interviewed guest on prime-time TV, but he really didn't know much about Israeli popular culture. Just as Bonnie had once introduced Yechiel to the New York cultural scene, Joelle showed him how to slow down and appreciate the pleasures of living in a Mediterranean country—a beer in a seaside café, an evening stroll along the water, a visit to an Israeli art gallery. She accepted that he was a man without hobbies or diversions, obsessed by his mission in the world and the thoughts in his head. He was good with her kids, generous and kind, good-looking (it mattered to her too), demonstratively grateful that she took him as he was. They were married in 2007. Under the bridal canopy, in a burst of unself-conscious joy, Eckstein turned to the guests and said, in a tone filled with amazement, "She loves me sooo much!"

Eckstein had barely settled into Jerusalem when he decided on a new American venture, an advocacy group known as Stand for Israel. After 9/11, President George W. Bush and his foreign-policy team were in no mood to condemn Israel for defending itself against Muslim terrorists. Bush, in fact, regarded Prime Minister Ariel Sharon as a mentor on the subject. Still, as always, there was political work to do in the United States to shore up Christian support for Israel. The mainline churches, increasingly in thrall to their pro-Palestinian activists, sought to portray themselves as the true voice of American Christianity. Eckstein appealed to his followers to let their congressional representatives know that evangelical Zionism was alive and stronger than ever. He encouraged them to mount media campaigns against what he saw as biased coverage of the Israeli-Arab conflict, and to support the Israeli economy by visiting and buying locally made products. He also launched the International Day of Prayer and Solidarity with Israel in some twenty thousand churches around the world.

Prayer and local messaging were all very nice, but Eckstein wanted to get back into the advocacy game. In 2003, he and Ralph Reed convened a two-day Stand for Israel briefing at the Mayflower Hotel in Washington, DC. Christian Zionists from all over the country gathered to listen to speeches by a galaxy of legislators, meet at the White House with mid-level officials (who assured them that relations with Israel had never been better), and attend a gala banquet honoring Democrat Tom Lantos, the only Holocaust survivor in Congress, and Republican majority leader Tom DeLay. As with the Center for Jewish and Christian Values, Eckstein attempted to keep Stand for Israel bipartisan (at the next event, the honorees were Republican Rudy Giuliani and Democratic senator Joe Lieberman), but it wasn't easy. Pro-Israel senators and congress members felt more at home at AIPAC conventions.

In truth, Eckstein felt ambivalent about Stand for Israel. As the Fellowship grew, demands on his time had increased. He was now a member of the executive committee of the Jewish Agency, charged with the aliyah portfolio, although he was, from the start, uneasy with that organization's lack of transparency and Byzantine internal politics. He was also on the board of the Joint Distribution Committee, and active in the former Soviet Union. Prime Minister Sharon made him an adviser and appointed him to the post of goodwill ambassador with an emphasis on Latin America—a ceremonial job but one that required considerable travel. The operation in Chicago was growing so fast that the Fellowship had to keep renting bigger offices.

Only his Washington, DC, efforts were disappointing. As usual, he blamed it on his inability to find good staff. Whatever the cause, there was a vacuum, and in 2006, Pastor John Hagee, a Pentecostal preacher from San Antonio, filled it by restarting a dormant Christian Zionist lobbying group called Christians United for Israel (CUFI). To bolster his clout in DC, he hired David Brog, the former chief of staff to Republican senator Arlen Specter. Brog, a graduate of Princeton and Harvard Law (and the cousin of Ehud Barak) was exactly the kind of executive Eckstein spent his professional lifetime unable to find. He knew how to operate in Washington, DC, and to leverage the power that Hagee, a popular television preacher, could bring to evangelical support for Israel.

The Eckstein-Hagee relationship goes back to the days when Yechiel was a young comer and Hagee, a former college football player and a fifth-generation minister of the gospel, was an ardent Zionist. When the two met, at a meeting of the National Religious Broadcasters, Hagee was in the process of establishing a Pentecostal megachurch and a television ministry that grew into a multichannel empire. Hagee invited Eckstein, who was ten years his junior, to speak at his church in San Antonio, and though the proposed engagement never took place, they stayed in touch.

In 2007, Hagee published a book about Christian-Jewish relations that led some evangelicals to accuse him of preaching "dual covenant" theology—that the Jews, as the chosen people, had their own, separate covenant with God, and didn't need to accept Jesus as the Messiah to gain salvation. Hagee, an abrasive man with lots of detractors, was concerned that his reputation was being tarnished, and he indignantly denied that he believed any such thing. After Jerry Falwell privately mocked him as "all hat and no cattle," Hagee reached out to Eckstein, asking him to help defuse the situation. Eckstein set up a conference call with Falwell, and Hagee deferentially explained that he did not in any way mean to imply that Jews didn't require salvation through Jesus. He merely meant that Christians shouldn't actively target Jews for conversion but act as witnesses for Jesus in their daily lives and let the Lord work his will. This was the position that Falwell and Eckstein had developed in tandem over the previous few years, and Falwell pronounced it acceptable. The conversation ended with pledges of mutual understanding. Eckstein felt that he had helped Hagee save his reputation and congratulated himself on another successful bridge-building effort.

When Falwell died the following year, Eckstein went to the funeral in Lynchburg, Virginia, in his capacity as Israel's goodwill ambassador. He was seated with other dignitaries in the front row, and after the service he gave a statement to the media praising Falwell's contributions to Israel and the Jewish people.

Hagee, who wanted very much to succeed Falwell as the leader of Christian Zionism, was seated ten rows back. When Eckstein walked over to greet some of the other mourners, he was surprised that Hagee didn't say hello or even make eye contact. Soon after, Hagee, through a staff member, asked the Fellowship to remove his picture and message of support from the Fellowship's promotional material.

Not long afterward, Eckstein and Hagee were scheduled to speak at the same church in Muncie, Indiana. Before the event, Eckstein schmoozed with his fellow dignitaries in the greenroom, but Hagee didn't join them. Eckstein was the first speaker, and he lavishly praised Hagee for the work he was doing on behalf of Israel and the Jewish people. Hagee didn't follow suit. "He didn't even acknowledge me," says Eckstein. "The way he snubbed me, I understood that he saw me not as a partner in a shared mission but as competition." Unlike the Fellowship, CUFI doesn't raise money for Israeli philanthropy. Its activities are concentrated on lobbying, campus advocacy for Israel, and holding annual events to educate and train Christian Zionist activists. John Hagee Ministries, a separate entity, does raise and distribute funds for Israel, although the amounts are minuscule.

Both CUFI and the Fellowship officially support any elected government in Israel, but Hagee is much more hawkish than Eckstein on Israeli territorial issues, and also far more incendiary in his public pronouncements. In 2006, on NPR's *Fresh Air*, Hagee remarked

that if only 15 percent of the world's 1.3 billion Muslims were mobilized to crush Israel, the resulting force would number 200
million—"far more than Hitler and Japan and Italy and all of the
Axis powers in World War II had under arms." Two years later, he
offended Catholics by insinuating that the church is anti-Semitic,
and he subsequently apologized for the remarks to the Catholic
League for Religious and Civil Rights.

Despite such controversies, and his very hard line on domestic
social issues, Hagee was embraced by the Jewish establishment in a
way that Eckstein had never been. "He goes to AIPAC conventions
and gets standing ovations. I've never been invited to speak at a
plenary session (or, for that matter, a session of the General Assembly of the Jewish Federations of North America). The first time
Hagee was invited to AIPAC I said to my board of directors, 'Okay.
Perhaps God is calling him to that role and not me.'" God was right.
At that point, Eckstein simply didn't have the time or energy to lead
the Christian Zionist lobby in the United States. Giving up DC
meant he could concentrate on Israel, where he was rapidly becoming an essential adjunct of the government.

In July 2006, Hezbollah fighters ambushed an Israeli patrol along
the northern border, killing three soldiers and capturing two more.
The Israeli government, led by Ehud Olmert, reacted with an invasion. For a month, Hezbollah fired Syrian-supplied rockets at Israeli
cities in the north; the IDF responded with air strikes and eventually a ground operation, which devastated much of south Lebanon
but didn't decisively defeat the guerrillas. Until the UN brokered a

ceasefire in mid-August, more than 300,000 Israelis in the Galilee were forced southward to escape rocket attacks. Those who remained had to huddle in filthy shelters, which lacked basic supplies or protection from the blistering Middle Eastern summer heat. The government in Jerusalem, safely out of missile range, seemed oblivious to the suffering of its citizens.

Eckstein saw what was happening and mobilized. He launched a fund-raising drive in the United States, with advertising on Fox News as well as on his usual channels. Meanwhile, he began writing checks for emergency supplies. With the national government seemingly paralyzed, he dealt directly with the mayors of cities in the north, rushing them hot food, milk, baby formula and diapers, toys, and bulletproof vests and helmets for government aid workers. Keren installed air-conditioning units and fans in the shelters, and provided funds for people with special needs. After the fighting, it renovated thousands of public and private shelters and bought eight fire engines for future emergencies. In all, it was an outlay of $25 million, accomplished with virtually no red tape. Eckstein toured the north, making sure that the supplies got where they were supposed to go, and after the fighting died down, he donated funds to build 2,400 shelters. In the field, Eckstein was careful but undeterred. "The Talmud says, 'People doing good deeds will not suffer harm.'" He paused, considering. "But, of course, the Talmud also tells the story of a great rabbi who became a heretic when he saw a young boy fall off a ladder and die while performing a good deed. Both of those things were on my mind."

Eckstein's activity caught the media's attention. For the first time, the broad Israeli public focused on Keren and its leader. The press reported that the money was coming from American Christians, and for once there was no vocal opposition from Eckstein's Haredi critics, who were providing nothing in the way of aid. Journalists asked why it was being left to foreigners—Gentiles at that—to take care of Israelis under bombardment. The Olmert government, humiliated, announced that it would match Eckstein's shelter funds. There were American Jewish contributions too, raised in an emergency campaign, but that was expected. Twenty-five million dollars in wartime aid from evangelical Christians was both novel and historic.

Almost no one came out of the war in Lebanon with an intact reputation. Prime Minister Olmert's approval rating fell to 3 percent, as protests against his government broke out around the country, and an official investigation found him guilty of mismanaging the war (he was subsequently convicted on unrelated corruption charges stemming from his tenure as mayor of Jerusalem, and sentenced to a lengthy prison term). Defense Minister Amir Peretz lost his place as leader of the Labor Party and eventually left the party entirely. Worst of all, the IDF chief of staff Dan Halutz, a decorated former fighter pilot, was caught selling off his portfolio in the Tel Aviv stock market just three hours after the attack that precipitated the decision to go to war. The scandal caused him to leave his post.

The sorry performance of the Israeli leadership was a profound lesson in Eckstein's political education. He had come to Jerusalem in awe of the selfless sons of the pioneers who dominated politics and ran the government. He had watched them flounder. After 2006, he didn't make that mistake again. "I learned that it is simply wrong to rely on bureaucrats and politicians. Until then, I didn't understand that in partnership with the government you can wind up waiting forever. I realized that if I want to do something, I just had to go ahead and do it."

In 2005, Israel withdrew from the Gaza Strip. Prime Minister Ariel Sharon had concluded that the evacuation was necessary, both to alleviate international pressure and to rid Israel of its obligation to control an increasingly restive Palestinian population. The departure from Gaza meant that thousands of Israeli settlers were forced to move. Some went willingly, but others refused. The evacuation, which was televised, involved some physical confrontations with the IDF soldiers, and many Israelis protested. Eckstein didn't join them, though he knew that many of his donors regarded this as a retreat from the Jewish patrimony. He maintained his policy of supporting every Israeli government. Moreover, he wasn't certain that leaving the Strip was a mistake.

On the Palestinian issue Eckstein has consistently attempted to avoid politics. His position is that he will support the foreign and defense policies of any elected government—though personally he is far more moderate than the majority of his donors. "I felt and still feel that Jews have the right to live in Judea and Samaria," he says. "But that doesn't mean necessarily living under Israeli sovereignty. I have no commitment to settlements being under Israeli flags. If the security issue is settled, I'd be for a Palestinian state."

There was much talk after the Israelis' departure from Gaza that the Palestinians would demonstrate their declared willingness to coexist peacefully, and set a comforting precedent for an eventual withdrawal from the West Bank. That didn't happen. The PLO rulers tore down every vestige of Jewish settlement, even those, like agricultural hothouses, that would have been useful. Then Hamas seized control in an armed overthrow, and rockets and bombs began falling on Israeli towns and villages along the border. Political pressure mounted on Jerusalem to respond. In December 2008 the IDF entered Gaza in an operation to wipe out the missile threat. The operation was code-named Cast Lead. In its early stages, it brought on an intensified Palestinian barrage. Missiles rained down on towns and cities as far away as the port of Ashdod. Schools were closed, businesses shuttered, and thousands of civilians fled. Civil defense arrangements were barely better than they had been in the 2006 Lebanon War. Eckstein visited the front lines and once again provided emergency aid, and fortified homes and public buildings. As Palestinians accused Israel of war crimes, Eckstein ran a public relations campaign in the United States to counter the charges. In all, the Fellowship spent about $2 million for advocacy and material support during Operation Cast Lead.

Eckstein's security reach was not restricted to Israel. He worked with the Foreign Ministry on advocacy. He coordinated with Israeli and American security organizations to provide protection for Jewish institutions overseas. After a terrorist attack on a synagogue and

Jewish campus in Turkey, the Fellowship contributed $750,000 to shore up its security system. When an attack on a Chabad house in Mumbai killed six, the Fellowship expanded its efforts to underwrite security for Chabad's houses and emissaries around the world. Eckstein was happy to make these contributions, but angry that much of this work fell to Christian donors. "The world Jewish community is so wealthy that it is a *shonda* [disgrace] that poor or threatened Jews—not just in Israel but in Russia, Ukraine, India, Morocco, all around the world—are left to shift for themselves. Christians donate sacrificially and give up luxuries to help Jews. And the Jewish community barely does anything."

Even as Eckstein was working against political violence abroad, he was experiencing it himself in Israel. About the same time Rabbi Porush had started going after Eckstein in the media, the campaign against him turned violent. One of his few black-hat supporters was a Haredi activist named Dudi Zilbershlag, who wanted to set up a Jerusalem soup kitchen in honor of his recently deceased fourteen-year-old son. Eckstein pledged a million dollars, and asked that a plaque identifying the Fellowship's Christian donors be placed on the building, a condition Zilbershlag met. Not long after opening its doors, the soup kitchen was stoned, windows broken, and the Fellowship plaque defaced. Zilbershlag became a target, and a few years later he fell into a honey trap, which was duly photographed. "He was caught in the act of being a human being," says Eckstein. "He's my friend; I don't judge him."

Eckstein himself became a target. Posters with threatening messages were hung in ultra-Orthodox neighborhoods, and his new wife, Joelle, received letters warning that she was in danger for consorting with a known missionary. The Shin Bet, Israel's FBI, told him to take the threats seriously and file a police report. He didn't, but Jerusalem cops began special patrols in his neighborhood anyway. The Fellowship board in Chicago encouraged him to hire bodyguards, which he declined to do. He did construct a security perimeter around his house. He also considered buying a gun, but decided against it. The idea of shooting at others, especially fellow Jews, even in self-defense, was too much for him to seriously contemplate.

In 2008, a Purim holiday package was delivered to the home of an American messianic pastor in the West Bank town of Ariel. When the pastor's fifteen-year-old son, Ami, tried to open the package, it exploded; it was a disguised bomb, filled with nails, screws, and needles, and the boy was badly injured. Police investigated and concluded that it had been a terrorist attack by ultra-Orthodox Jews. Eckstein stepped up his security, especially after visiting Ami in the hospital. "I didn't know the family. I don't approve of missionary activity toward Jews. But I went as a rabbi, to express outrage at the attack and to provide whatever comfort I could."

The gesture was not much noted in the American evangelical community, and in any case, for some of Eckstein's friends it was too little, too late. One of them was Pastor Jack Hayford. He had never pushed to aggressively pursue Jewish conversions, but discrimination against Christians was another matter. "I began to hear reports that messianic Christians were being persecuted by the Orthodox in Israel," he says. "There are anti-missionary campaigns going on. And I know that Rabbi Eckstein has a policy of not contributing to the causes of messianic Christians. And so I have asked to no longer be included in the Fellowship's infomercials and other publicity." Hayford informed Eckstein that the decision wasn't personal. "I understand the pressure Yechiel is under in Israel, and I still respect and love him," he says. It is a nicer rejection than the ones Eckstein has received from the rabbinical establishment, but no less painful. Eckstein's effort to combine Orthodox Judaism with Christian Zionism has put him in the paradoxical position of being rejected as a Christian missionary by the rabbinical establishment, and as an anti–Christian missionary activist by Christian Zionists like Hayford, Dobson, and Paige Patterson.

Despite all the criticism, the Fellowship continued to flourish. In 2012 it took in $118 million in the United States and Canada. In 2013, there was a slight dip to $116 million, but by the end of 2014, contributions reached $138 million and are projected to hit $180 million by the end of 2015. As far as Eckstein is concerned, this is a drop in the bucket. There are, according to the Pew-Templeton Global Religious Futures Project, 869 million evangelical, Charismatic, and Pentecostal Christians in the world, a majority of them outside the United States and Canada. China alone has an estimated 67 million Christians, a large portion of them evangelicals. Pentecostal Christianity is successfully competing with Catholicism throughout Latin America too. In Brazil, which has the largest Christian population outside the United

States, roughly 20 percent of believers now identify as Charismatics, Pentecostals, and evangelicals. So do a majority of Nigeria's eighty million Christians. Seoul, South Korea, has the world's biggest Christian congregation: the Yoido Full Gospel Church, with more than one million members.

This is too much potential to be ignored. In the summer of 2013, Eckstein paid a visit to South Korea, where he spoke at several major Christian venues. He was so encouraged by the response that he has opened an office in Seoul, as well as Israel, the United States, Canada, Ukraine, Australia, and Brazil.

Eckstein's radio ministry, *Holy Land Moments*, broadcast on over 2,900 stations around the world, is heard by an estimated seventeen million listeners a week. Since the launch of *Momentos en Tierra Santa* in 2012, perhaps a third of them are listening in Spanish. These programs emphasize the Jewish roots of Christianity.

One summer day in 2013, Eckstein was sitting at an open-air café near his Jerusalem office when Matan Vilnai happened by. Vilnai, a retired general and former cabinet minister, was then Israel's ambassador to China. He was in Jerusalem on a visit. That day he had dropped his wife off for an appointment in the neighborhood, stopped to get some pizza, and spotted Eckstein. Over kosher slices Eckstein told Vilnai of his successful Korean trip. "There are fourteen million Christians there," said Eckstein. "Isn't that amazing?"

"Of course, there aren't that many Christians in China," said Vilnai. "Only a hundred million." Eckstein smiled; he has a very accurate idea of how many Christians live in China, but he also knows how attached former generals are to one-upmanship. "You should come to China," Vilnai said. "I can open up the entire country for you."

"I wish I had the staff for it," said Eckstein.

"Keep it in mind," Vilnai said, standing to go. "The offer is always open. Come to China and the embassy will help you."

Eckstein sighed, just thinking about the effort. His international expansion had taken a lot out of him. He was exhausted and overextended already, but a combination of fervor and personal ambition forced him to at least contemplate the opportunity. "It is logical that we could be bringing in a billion dollars a year within five to seven years from evangelicals around the world who love Israel," he said. "This isn't a goal in a formal sense, but I'm sure it's true. And there is a lot of use for the money. For every one of the projects we do now, there are five or six I have to say no to. I'd love to have enough to provide dental care to the elderly, for example; or help people with physical handicaps. We need funds for so many things." Eckstein paused, looking out at the Jerusalem landscape he loved and didn't get to see enough. He had built spiritual bridges across millennia of misunderstanding and animosity (and traversed personal bridges of his own, from his Canadian boyhood to New York, from the warmth of the Orthodox yeshiva world to the pulpits of forbidden megachurches, from his home with Bonnie and the girls to a new life in Israel). At some point he would have to stop, settle down with his new wife and grandchildren. A part of him wanted to do that now. But he was too restless and too driven to make such a decision. Life had taught him to leave things in the hands of God. He would provide the next challenge. He always had.

Thirteen

❖

UNDER FIRE

In 2008, Hamas rocket fire from Gaza once again became intolerable, and the IDF crossed the border in force to stop it. This time, though, the civilian population was less exposed than it had been during the Lebanese incursion or previous Gaza operations. The Israeli antiaircraft system known as Iron Dome got its first operational test, and it passed spectacularly. Palestinians fired 1,128 rockets. More than a quarter were shot down; most of the others landed harmlessly. Still, being fired upon was a traumatic experience for civilians.

Eckstein spent much of the war on the front lines, helping affected communities and documenting the fighting. "At night along the Strip, the incoming rockets were like a fireworks display," recalls Lynn Doerschuk. "Missiles flying, the Iron Dome batteries firing, sirens sounding. We were filming near the town of Sderot, right near the border, and we spotted four armed Palestinians just across the field. Yechiel was in the middle of doing his stand-up when the sirens went off and we heard gunshots. Yechiel dived for the ground as the bullets went right over our heads. When the shooting stopped, he got up and began talking again as if nothing happened."

On one particularly hot day, Eckstein toured on the battlefield with Avi Dichter, the former head of the Shin Bet secret service and, at the time, a cabinet minister. The laconic spy chief and the voluble rabbi had forged a friendship over seven years of working together on security matters. In a letter, Dichter praised Eckstein's courage and self-possession under fire from "tens of rockets." Being recognized as a comrade-in-arms was a special moment for Eckstein—better than the symbolic dog tags he received or the awards he gets from groups he helps, such as the Friends of the Israel Defense Forces (FIDF).

General Yitzhak Gershon, a former Israeli commander, was the American point man for FIDF. In the spring of 2013 he came to the New York Hilton to discuss money. He is the kind of soldier Yechiel dreamed of becoming—a brash sabra with a hail-fellow-well-met persona. Most Israeli general officers do academic training in engineering or the sciences; Gershon has a degree in public relations.

At a table in the coffee shop, Gershon quickly ran down the aid for needy soldiers his organization had received from the Fellowship in the previous year: holiday baskets of food for the soldiers and their families, allowances for civilian clothing, and direct funding for personal and family expenses. "There are three thousand soldiers who have been able to remain in the army because of your help," he told Eckstein. "I talked to the director general today and he personally asked me to tell you that."

"Wonderful," said Eckstein, beaming.

"Next year we want to expand our aid, take care of more soldiers," Gershon said. "We are hoping for one million dollars from you."

Eckstein nodded. "All right."

"But," said Gershon, as though he had just thought of it, "you can't have a program like this for just one year. It has to be continuous."

"That's true," Eckstein said.

"So I'm going to ask you to commit to a million dollars a year for five years," said Gershon. They had been speaking in Hebrew, but for this he switched to English. Sometimes it is easier to ask for money in somebody else's language. Eckstein is aware of that; he recalls with distaste his own early years at the Fellowship, begging millionaires for a few thousand dollars. He smiled at Gershon and said, "You got it. Anything else?"

Gershon rolled up his shirtsleeve. "The hair on my arm is standing up," he said.

Eckstein glanced. If there were hairs standing at attention, they weren't visible. "Fine," he said. "Anything else you need from me?"

"That's more than enough," Gershon said.

Eckstein rose and extended his hand. Gershon gave it a soldierly pump. "You missed your chance," Eckstein said warmly. "You could have asked for more." A few months later, at a gala in Los Angeles, he announced a contribution to the FIDF of $4.5 million. He went up onstage and entertained the crowd with a Hebrew song, sharing the bill with Lionel Richie. "He was pretty good too," says Eckstein with a smile.

In the summer of 2013, Eckstein drove down to the Negev desert to visit the IDF's newly opened fire-training center, and to present a group of reserve soldiers with a gift: an armored welcome wagon, equipped with phones and Internet access to help soldiers in the field stay in touch with the outside world; a drop-down side screen that served as an outdoor cinema; a canteen for snacks and drinks; and a portable picnic area with tables and chairs on a lawn of green Astroturf. The price tag was half a million dollars. Eckstein was footing half the bill. The other half was paid for by an Israeli NGO headed by a former brigadier general, Avigdor Kahalani.

A couple of reservist platoons sat under canvas tarps in the intense desert heat, waiting for the presentation to begin. They were a cross section of Israel's ethnically diverse populace—black Ethiopians, brown Yemenites, pale Russians, wizened Bedouin scouts, some soldiers wearing yarmulkes, others with tattoos on their necks and forearms. A plague of locusts was sweeping the Negev, and while they waited, the soldiers flicked them off their uniforms. An officer recalled the locusts God sent against Pharaoh to spur the exodus from Egypt. "That was three thousand years ago," he said, "and here we are again, back in the desert, all over again."

Eckstein, dressed casually in a golf shirt and khakis, was introduced. He apologized in good Hebrew for his poor Hebrew and told the soldiers that money for the vehicle had come from "Christians in America who support Israel." There was polite applause. "No, you are the ones who deserve applause," he said. "You are the salt of the earth. Everything this vehicle dispenses—coffee and soda, food, a place to rest in comfort—are things you've earned."

Avigdor Kahalani followed Eckstein. As a young tank commander in the 1973 Yom Kippur War, he had more or less single-handedly stopped a Syrian armored force from overrunning a sector of the Golan Heights. Kahalani left the army as a brigadier general, went into politics, found it wasn't for him, and took over the NGO. Gesturing at the welcome wagon, he recalled how happy soldiers would have been in the old days to have a motorized oasis like this one, and how grateful they would have been to a patron like Eckstein. "He's the only rabbi in the world who could have gone to Christians, raised money, and brought it here!" The applause was once again mild—really, it was too hot for enthusiasm—and Kahalani admonished them to express some real gratitude. "If you can't clap any louder than that, no Christian will ever send you another gift," he said.

"Don't worry," Eckstein called from his seat in the front row. "Just tell me what you need."

"We could use another welcome wagon," said Kahalani.

"You got it," Eckstein called out and made a note on his omnipresent recorder.

As the Fellowship played a larger and larger role in Israeli life, Eckstein's greatest effect came not through the army or the national government, but through mayors. In the Israeli system, mayors are strictly local. They don't control the police, the fire department, or, for the most part, the schools. Those budgets are allocated by the national government. What small-town mayors have is a grassroots connection to their constituents, which means direct contact with people in trouble. Since social welfare budgets are modest, finding outside funding is especially important. A cabinet minister in Jerusalem might turn down financial help for ideological reasons, but few mayors—Jewish or Arab, ultra-Orthodox or anti-Zionist—are in a position to be so principled.

Working with mayors, Keren established social welfare projects in 170 towns and villages, 48 of them Arab, 122 Jewish—every place in Israel at the sixtieth percentile and lower on the national measure of standard of living. "Our funds are twice what the national government gives to the mayors for emergency funds," he says. "We work through the mayors because they know how to get things done and where the money needs to go. In poor towns, people go to city hall for help. And the mayors know they can rely on us to come through, quickly."

Not everyone is a fan of this method. Among the critics is Bob Asher, the former chairman of the IFCJ board. "Yechiel has money and a sense of where it should go to help people," he says. "As chairman, I didn't like the process, especially the emergency funds to mayors. Yechiel was more or less personally deciding how to distribute the money."

Eckstein doesn't necessarily disagree. He has learned in a decade of trial and error that the mayors of Israel are a mixed bag: some are honest, others less so. To prevent abuses he has instituted a series of strict accounting measures and practices. One safeguard is the practice of making three payments a year, and seeing to it that new funds are not released until the previous portion is fully accounted for. Eckstein isn't under the illusion that mayors are a perfect vehicle for his activities, but they do have a political interest in helping him get money to the needy. "Often people ask me, 'Why is this your responsibility?' That's a good question. The Ministry of Social Welfare should do it. But I have to make a choice. Do I leave the kids without shoes and say it's the national government's obligation? Or do I help them get shoes? Dental care? Food for the holidays? I don't work with a budget. I try to raise as much money as I can and distribute it in the best ways I can. Could I find a better way? I'm working on that. But in the meantime, you have to take care of people. You can't just let them suffer until you come up with perfect bureaucratic solutions." That realization was a major step forward. He was no longer the awed idealistic newcomer to Israel. Experience had made him a realist.

And the experience just keeps growing. Eckstein's office in Jerusalem gets roughly sixty requests a month. On a Wednesday in July, Eckstein and two senior staff members went over a list. The first was from Nir Barkat, the mayor of Jerusalem. Barkat is an Israeli Mike Bloomberg, a high-tech multimillionaire who went into politics late in his career. His relationship with Eckstein is well established and encompasses a large number of ventures. Most of them are standard social welfare issues, but two years ago the mayor asked Eckstein to rescue Beitar Jerusalem, the city's iconic soccer team. The team has a nominal connection to the Likud, and many of its fans are Likud voters; they also have a reputation for being soccer thugs. Lately Beitar had fallen on hard economic times, and was in danger of collapsing. Losing it would be bad for the morale of the city, Barkat said. Could Eckstein prop up the team?

Keren established four categories of aid: immigration, resettlement, welfare, and security. Money goes to every segment of Israelis in need. Saving a soccer team fell within none of these. Still, Eckstein has considerable leeway and a good imagination. He suggested that Beitar's after-school program for kids be expanded to emphasize good sportsmanship and tolerance, and opened to poor children who couldn't afford the fee. In return, Keren would agree to pay $750,000 over two years. And so it did.

But there were two other professional soccer teams in Jerusalem, Ha'Poel and Ha'Poel Katamon, both suffering financially and both connected in high places. A senior official in the prime minister's office had contacted Eckstein with a request for a bailout. One of Prime Minister Netanyahu's chief fund-raisers, it turned out, was also chairman of Ha'Poel. Once more Eckstein agreed, on the condition that the other teams follow the same educational program. But there was no noticeable uptick in sportsmanship on the playing fields of Jerusalem, and after a while Eckstein stopped the donations.

Today there was another sports request on the agenda. Barkat wanted to stage an international teen-sports competition in Jerusalem. It would be an opportunity for the mayor to showcase the capital's new sports facility. That, in turn, would require a full house of enthusiastic fans. But it wasn't at all clear that a crowd would turn up to watch a bunch of foreign kids engage in relay races and the javelin toss, so city hall wanted Eckstein to buy tickets for the event and give them out to schoolchildren. Eckstein heard this request with a frown. It was an "ask" too far. "Send them a no," he instructed one of his aides. "A nice no. Where are we on the homeless shelter in Jerusalem?"

"Barkat's office is working on it," said the aide.

"That's not acceptable," said Eckstein. "We've been waiting for an answer for a year and a half. What are people supposed to do, sleep in the street? I want to do something about this right now!"

The aide reminded him that Keren was still renting a Jerusalem hotel for the homeless. Eckstein was not mollified. "I want to pressure them for a real solution," he said. "In that letter to the mayor about the tickets, add a PS. Tell him that after we take care of the homeless we can turn our attention to trivial requests like this. Tell him we are waiting for action." He paused, looking at his staffers. "And let me see that letter before you send it out."

For years, Eckstein had a significant adversary in the realm of Israeli social action: ultra-Orthodox officials who controlled the government ministries in charge of health, education, and welfare; they largely weren't interested in cooperating with him. That changed with the election in 2013, which gave birth to a nearly unprecedented Haredi-free coalition, led by Prime Minister Netanyahu. Yair Lapid, who became minister of finance in the new government, was an author, a journalist, and a former prime-time TV host; he was also the head of a new party dedicated to moderating the power of religion in government. Over the years, he and Eckstein became close friends. Lapid has an autistic daughter, and at his behest, Eckstein donated a million dollars for an autism clinic. In the run-up to the 2013 election, Eckstein considered joining Lapid's party as he had once considered a run for the Senate in Illinois—he would almost certainly have won a seat in the Knesset—but in the end he decided to maintain his nonpartisan status. Still, he was delighted by his friend's electoral success and the rise of his Yesh Atid party, which now took control of the Ministry of Social Welfare and the Ministry of Education. Soon after the election, Eckstein held a round of meetings with the new cabinet ministers to explore ways of working through the national government.

At the time, Israel's Channel 2 TV was making a documentary film on Eckstein and his charities, and a crew accompanied him to his meeting with Meir Cohen, the recently appointed minister of social welfare. Cohen was the former mayor of Dimona, a small and not especially affluent town in the Negev desert, and he had a long association with Eckstein, which he happily recounted for the camera.

"When I came into office in Dimona, I discovered that there was no doctor in town. Not a single one. And there was no money to hire one. I called Rabbi Eckstein. He told me, 'I'll come to Dimona next month, and you will have a doctor.' A month later he came, we toured the city, and he saw for himself that we had no medical clinic. So he built one, a beautiful place that serves the entire town. No bureaucracy, no waiting, just doing what was necessary. He built us a great youth center too—it became a model for others all around the country. That's the Rabbi Eckstein I know."

Eckstein thanked Cohen for thanking him and then got down to business. "As you know," he said, "we spend $40 million every year for welfare projects. Our donors are non-Jews. And I have to tell you, sometimes I am embarrassed by the situation here, the gaps between rich and poor and the extent of poverty."

Eckstein's Guardians of Israel fund-raising is based on graphically depicting this poverty. The images make many Israelis and American Jewish Zionists cringe, and even some of Eckstein's evangelical supporters feel he goes too far. "I have a concern about the fact that a lot of Yechiel's mailings and television almost present Israel as a Third World country—the starving people of Israel and all that," says Jerry Rose, one of the original mainstays of the Fellowship. "The telecasts are brilliant at eliciting empathy. But the message can make things seem worse than they are."

Eckstein disagrees. In his view, the infomercials and direct mail are forceful expressions of reality. Just a few days before his meeting with Cohen, the Organisation for Economic Co-operation and Development published its annual national survey, in which Israel was listed as the poorest of the developed nations, with greater social inequality than China or Mexico.

"I'm here to tell you today that you and the government are not alone. We are with you," Eckstein said to Cohen. "We've got your back."

"Thank you," Cohen said, glancing at the camera. Cabinet

ministers can always use publicity, but at the same time there would be viewers who didn't like it and commentators who would mock the government for needing backup from a private charity.

Eckstein wanted to focus his work with the ministry on care for the elderly, with a secondary priority given to young people. Cohen had a different agenda. He argued that the situation of the elderly actually wasn't bad—they had national pensions and other programs to rely on. "The problems of the elderly are important, obviously, and whatever you can do will be wonderful. No question about it. But the mayors already have the means to feed the elderly. We have a more serious issue with at-risk youth."

It wasn't clear if Cohen was commiserating with the old folks or disagreeing with Eckstein because he wanted viewers to see that the minister of social welfare had a mind of his own. Eckstein chose to interpret the gesture as commiseration, but he was firm. "There are 200,000 hungry elderly in Israel," he said. "We have budgeted 100 million shekels [roughly $35 million] for them this year. We'll give out food cards for 21,000 meals a week. If they can't get out of the house, we will send the food to them. If they can't fix the food, someone will prepare it for them. We are also going to arrange for heating and we'll distribute credit cards that will take care of whatever co-pays national health insurance doesn't cover. And we will set up home visits by volunteers to relieve people's sense of isolation. That's our plan."

"Well, excellent," said Cohen. It wasn't his money, after all. Old people did need taking care of, and whatever he saved this way could be used for other purposes. Christian, Jewish—money is fungible.

Eckstein now turned to Cohen's main concern. Keren would provide $2 million to repair and maintain halfway houses and dormitories for kids who had been removed from their families. Not only that, there would be millions more for sending fifty thousand poor and needy kids to summer day camps throughout the country.

"Arabs as well as Jews?" asked Cohen.

"Of course," Eckstein said.

"Excellent," said the minister, consulting his watch.

"I also want to mention our program for foster children," said Eckstein. "Right now, 75 percent of kids at risk are in dormitory programs and only one-quarter in foster families. Social research tells us that foster families are much better solutions. We want to provide the funds to reverse the ratio, make it 75 percent foster families and only 25 percent dormitories."

The minister looked surprised. He hadn't been briefed on this. A ministry adviser, who had survived many ministers and many improvement schemes, objected. "Fixing up dilapidated dormitories, fine. Summer camps for the kids, great. But sending kids to foster homes is a multiyear commitment. You can't put kids somewhere for a year and then maybe run out of money. Somebody has to pay for it."

"You are absolutely right," said Eckstein. "I agree that there hasn't been enough coordination in recent years between us and the Ministry of Social Welfare. But that can change, now. And don't worry about the funding. We'll keep it going." There were nods all around and smiles all around. Who turns down free money?

When the documentary was shown, it caused a stir. *Yediot Aharonot,*

Israel's most influential newspaper, interviewed Eckstein and asked a provocative question: Were he and his Christian Zionist donors replacing the Israeli government as a provider of social services?

That suggestion infuriated people at the Ministry of Social Welfare, who anonymously accused Eckstein of being a glory hound.

It is a common accusation. Eckstein is aggressive in promoting his group's activities and his own "brand." He appears on prime-time television shows to discuss his activities and runs radio spots whose thickly American-accented greeting—"Shalom, this is Rabbi Yechiel Eckstein from the Keren L'Yedidut"—is endlessly imitated and often snickered at by Tel Aviv sophisticates. Eckstein knows that some Israelis find his Zionist sincerity off-putting or consider him a glory seeker, but he dismisses this as the price of letting Israelis know that the Christian Zionists are their friends and benefactors. For the same reason, he insists that soup kitchens, social centers, old-age homes, hospital wings, and dormitories sponsored by the Fellowship display plaques identifying the source of the charity.

"Honors and recognition are part of fund-raising," he points out. "The trick is not to get to where you need them." It is a trick, Eckstein concedes, that he has not fully mastered. His successes have not sated his insecurities and his hungers. Over the years, he has hired (and fired) a depressingly large number of public relations gurus and advertising geniuses to get recognition for his message and his personal brand. Recently, while debating a proposal that he underwrite a show on social welfare on Israeli TV, he called a friend for advice. "Be honest with me," he said. "If I do this, will it be because of my ego, my need for fame, my desire to be recognized by the public, or is it really out of a pure motive of getting the message out?" He ruminates on this question often, sometimes in public, as though his own motives were a mystery to him. The friend reminded him that even Moshe Maimonides, the most venerated Jewish thinker of the Middle Ages, famous for praising charity given in secret, put his own name on the cover of his books.

When a hotel maid recognized Eckstein in New York, and said she was one of his devoted fans and contributors, he beamed for days. But his sensitivity works both ways. One summer day he was sitting at an outdoor café near his office in Jerusalem when a woman stopped at his table to ask for directions. The two struck up a conversation, and it turned out she was a tour guide who worked mostly with groups of Christian pilgrims to the Holy Land from Latin America.

"Do you ever work with groups from the US?" he asked.

"Sure," she said. "I just had one."

"Did anyone mention Keren L'Yedidut?"

She shook her head. "I don't know what that is," she said.

"It's a fellowship between Christians and Jews, run by Rabbi Yechiel Eckstein," said Rabbi Yechiel Eckstein hopefully.

The woman shook her head. "Never heard of him," she said.

After she was gone, Eckstein sighed. "All the effort we have put into bringing this into Israeli consciousness and putting Christian Zionist support on the map, and here is this woman—she *works* in the field and she hasn't heard of us. We are the biggest philanthropy in Israel and nobody knows who we are." This is a glum exaggeration.

Eckstein and his fund are very well known in the small, outlying towns of Israel, the poor neighborhoods of major cities, old-age homes, and immigrant absorption centers throughout the country—the places his charity reaches. In Jerusalem, and even in secular Tel Aviv, he is frequently stopped on the street by grateful beneficiaries, or given a honk and a thumbs-up from passing motorists. Eckstein often reminds himself that virtue is its own reward, there are limits to public relations, and no philanthropist is known by everyone. But hey, a rabbi can wish.

Fourteen

❖

"BEFORE YOU WERE BORN, WE CARED ABOUT YOU"

On a blistering day in mid-June, 2013, Eckstein flew to Moscow to inspect some of his Isaiah 58 projects. He had been on the road more or less continuously for days, flying back and forth between Chicago, Jerusalem, Kiev, and Moscow. Now he was sitting in a kosher restaurant a few miles from the Kremlin, eating a dinner that consisted mostly of meat—lamb chops, grilled chicken, and hamburger kebab, with a side of rice—ordered by his hosts, two Chabad operatives who were aware of Eckstein's famously carnivorous appetite. Joelle watched him tuck into the meal with resigned disapproval. Eckstein has stopped smoking cigarettes (several times), and he exercises to keep his weight down, but his heart condition hasn't had an appreciable impact on his wide-ranging appreciation of food.

Shabbat is Yechiel Eckstein's favorite day. In Jewish mysticism it is associated with the *Shekinah*, a feminine name for God. "The days of the week are masculine," says Eckstein. "The Shabbat is a queen. Shabbat provides completion, fullness, yin and yang. That's why it is valued more than other days. These days, Jewish culture places much too much emphasis on the God who creates, the dominating male principle, the importance of conquering the mountain. There is joy and wisdom in waiting for God to call you to another task, in resting as well as doing." And, when it comes to celebrating Shabbat, aside from Jerusalem there is no place he would rather do it than in Moscow.

This was Eckstein's sixteenth trip to the former Soviet Union, and he was there on business, to oversee some of the projects he funds across ten time zones on behalf of the 500,000 or so Jews who didn't emigrate after the fall of Communism. Over the years, the contributions to these projects have exceeded half a billion dollars, but Eckstein has no office in Russia. His home base for the visit was the Marina Roscha Synagogue and Jewish Community Center, owned and operated by the Chabad movement, Russia's most important Jewish organization.

Eckstein's hosts in Moscow that night were employees of the diamond magnate Lev Leviev, a major Chabad donor and a significant partner of Eckstein's in Russian philanthropy. Leviev was born in Tashkent in 1956, moved to Israel in 1971, and dropped out of school to help support the family as a diamond cutter. He had steady hands (his hobby is ritual circumcision) and enormous self-confidence (his first patient was his eldest son). Over time, Leviev went from cutting diamonds to finding them and trading them; now one of the world's richest men, he owns mines across the globe and battles De Beers for dominance in the industry. For years Leviev tried unsuccessfully to rally American Jewish organizations to help with education in Russia—and then he met Eckstein. He was suspicious of the Christian connections, but when Eckstein came up with money, Leviev was convinced; the two became friends and partners in funding the Chabad's Russian Jewish school system.

Leviev gives Chabad millions each year through the Ohr Avner Foundation; Eckstein is also among the organization's major donors. In essence, the two men are partners in cradle-to-grave social services for Jews from the Turkish border to Siberia. They fund schools, summer camps, kosher food banks, medical clinics, old-age homes, and community centers. This work is carried out primarily by a network of Chabad emissaries, known in Yiddish-inflected Hebrew as *shluchim*.

The concept came from the Rebbe himself. In the early 1950s he handpicked a few of his most talented students, matched them with brides, and sent the young couples out into the world to bring Jews back to Orthodox Judaism. The job was a hard sell. Shluchim were (and are) sent wherever a rabbi is needed. That could be Los Angeles or Laos, Paris or Siberia—and almost every place seemed unwelcoming. The communities of Europe had been destroyed by the Holocaust. Behind the Iron Curtain, several million Jews were trapped in an oppressive empire where religion was banned. Israel was ruled by atheist socialists whose assumption was that Orthodoxy was a dying relic. In the United States, assimilation and social mobility were moving Jews out of their self-imposed ghettos into the liberal American mainstream. Sending out a few sheltered yeshiva boys in black hats, armed with a rudimentary secular education and a commission to change the tide of history, was a long shot. The conditions of service weren't especially promising, either. After a couple of years of support from the Chabad central office, they are expected to make their own living by fund-raising—and to put the money back into the local Jewish community, where they will stay for the rest of their lives. Shluchim start out as young idealists, but unlike Mormons or Peace Corps volunteers, they get old in the job.

Eckstein is deeply impressed by the hard work and self-sacrifice of the shluchim, each of whom gets financial support from the Fellowship via Isaiah 58. Eckstein personally pays the travel expenses of wives who accompany their husbands to Chabad's annual gathering in New York. "I wasn't raised in Chabad," he says. "But what these men and women are doing deserves respect and support. In the USSR, Jews never had a rabbi. They never set foot in a synagogue. Young people today are the third generation of the victims of Communism. At least their parents and grandparents, when they were growing up, had older relatives with memories of Jewish life. The third generation comes from homes with nothing. If they are lost to Judaism, they and their children will be lost forever. The shluchim are doing holy work."

Shabbat starts at sundown, which in early summer reaches Moscow at around 11:00 p.m. Eckstein and Joelle came to Marina Roscha early, to attend Chabad's weekly Gen X gathering. When they entered the room, they found an elegant dinner party about to begin. A hundred or so young singles sat at round tables, chatting over the sounds of a jazz quartet. Vodka and wine were poured from bottles set on every table. Social drinking on Shabbat and holidays is a Chabad tradition, and it is particularly useful as an icebreaker. The purpose of the Friday night dinner club is very clear—to encourage eligible young Jews to marry one another and raise Jewish families.

Most ultra-Orthodox Jews regard their secular counterparts with disdain and fear. Their world is closed, their gaze fixed inward and backward. Outsiders are unwelcome. Chabad is unique in its desire to missionize the unobservant. The shluchim are as personally Orthodox as any other black hats, but they have a more sophisticated acceptance of the world around them, and they use the sounds and tastes and currents of popular culture to make contact with the nonreligious. That's why the Friday night dinner menu was sushi, not gefilte fish. Both are kosher, but kosher isn't the same as cool.

In its missionizing, Chabad believes in taking it one day at a time. The Rebbe taught that Jews have souls whose inherent Jewishness can be awakened by a single religious act. Come to shul, drink a cocktail, dig some Miles, maybe say a blessing over the bread, maybe not—it's all good. The main thing is that you are in shul. There are no good Jews or bad Jews, just Jews who need a little help finding their essence, one mitzvah at a time.

This relaxed attitude extends to social arrangements. Seating at the dinner was mixed. Women wore fashionably revealing summer outfits, the men came in jeans and covered their heads with caps or stylish hats. The emcee was a well-known Russian entertainer who had given up his career to join Chabad. Wearing the shluchim uniform—black suit, prayer fringes hanging over the belt, and a beard—he crooned Sinatra songs and got laughs with in-jokes and topical wisecracks.

During a break in the music, Eckstein was introduced and asked to say a few words. He took the stage beaming. "You guys are so lucky," he said. "You've got the most beautiful women in the world right here!" The crowd laughed. They belong to the class of educated young Russians who understand English as a matter of course.

"In 1965, in New York, I took part in my first protest rally on behalf of the Jews of Russia," Eckstein said. "It was a sit-in at the Soviet consulate. I was in high school then, and our rabbis told us not to go, not to protest. I think that was the first time I ever went against the word of my rabbi. We sat on the sidewalk and chanted, 'One, two, three, four / Open up the iron door!' There were no synagogues like this in Moscow, then. There was no way for Jews to leave the USSR, or for us to come be with you. But here we are to-night, together, still Jewish despite everything. I think it is a miracle."

One of the shluchim brought a guitar to the stage and handed it to Eckstein. "Please sing a song," he said. "You never know when a soul will be touched." Eckstein, who does not suffer from stage fright, strummed the guitar and began singing "Shalah et Ami" (Let My People Go), an anthem of the Free Soviet Jewry movement. He sang in Russian and Hebrew, and the audience, too young to remember the song, clapped along. Then Eckstein broke into "Od Avinu Chai" (Our Father Still Lives), written by his friend Rabbi Shlomo Carlebach, the wandering bard who called Eckstein "my holy brother." The title alludes to the Torah story of Joseph's meeting with the brothers who sold him into Egyptian bondage. "Does my father still live?" Joseph asks. Carle-bach turned it into an affirmation—"our father still lives," and added the lyric "am Israel chai" (the people of Israel live). Few other songs so clearly express the post-Holocaust determination of the Jewish people to continue. "When I was a kid, I dreamed of becoming Shlomo Carlebach," Eckstein says. "He was my idol and then my mentor and most of all, my friend. Nobody can ever replace him in my life."

For Eckstein's generation of American Jews, the struggle to free Soviet Jewry was an epochal moment, ranking with Israel's victory in the Six-Day War. It offered a chance to reply "never again" to the Holocaust, to assert agency against an anti-Semitic empire. The fall of Communism was, for once, a happy ending, and to him the exodus from Russia to Israel *did* seem like a miracle, a fulfillment of biblical prophecy. One of the greatest moments of his life was bringing a Torah scroll to the Jews of Uzbekistan—the first one they had received since the establishment of the Soviet Union in 1917. He had been right to reject his rabbi, to protest and raise his voice. Here, sitting before him in this elegant room in a Moscow synagogue, was the proof. He strummed the last chord, put down the guitar, and said, "Before you were born, we cared about you. Before you were born, we didn't want to lose you." The antidepressant wasn't working that night; there were tears in his eyes when he left the stage. Joelle rose to greet him and, as they do each Shabbat, they embraced and held each other for a long moment. That, too, was extraordinary; Orthodox rabbis don't publicly display affection with their wives.

After dinner, he davened with the group in a small chapel, where the Chabadnik emcee held up signs in transliterated Hebrew for those who hadn't yet learned the prayers. Eckstein, of course, knew them by heart. Everyone wished one another "Shabbat shalom," and he and Joelle, accompanied by Shlomi Peles, the Israel-based Chabad rabbi who serves as one of Eckstein's key links to the organization, and a blond Gentile teenager whose job it was to work the elevator walked back to the hotel in the broad daylight of 10:00 p.m.

Eckstein was back in shul the following morning. Normally this is a chore for him—he hasn't felt comfortable in a synagogue since he was booted out of the Kollel in Chicago. He feels judged and gossiped about, a sense that deepened in Israel when he found himself persona non grata as an accused Christian missionary. He sometimes attends modern Orthodox shuls, but he finds the experience rote and arid.

Prayer to him is highly emotional and personal. A few years earlier, following a serious heart attack, he was allowed to leave the intensive care unit to attend Shabbat services, but when he got to the hospital synagogue, it was empty. "There I was, with a drip attached to my arm, all alone. That morning I felt an incredible davening. I started to cry—crying and prayer go together for me. During my divorce I cried out in pain. After I met Joelle I would daven outside in Jerusalem and tears of joy would run down my face because I felt completed. In the hospital I was crying because I recognized my mortality. I believe that there is a soul, a spirit that is part of God. Genesis calls it 'the breath of life.' I don't claim to know what happens to the spirit after it returns to God. Concepts of judgment, heaven, hell—I don't really think about those things. Do I sometimes doubt God? I have doubts every morning—it is the first thing I think about in my davening, my prayers. And every day, all over again, I re-create the feeling of God's presence in me. We say, in the first prayer of the morning, thanks to God for returning my soul to me, for allowing me to live another day."

Eckstein takes the words of his prayers seriously, even if he does edit them to fit his beliefs and doesn't mind innovating when necessary. He is a feminist (at least by Orthodox standards), and when his first daughter was born, in 1977, he created and performed a naming ceremony for her that took the place of the circumcision ceremony performed for sons. This was considered such a radical departure from tradition that the *New York Times* covered it. "All rabbis, including the Orthodox, agree that women share equally with men in the covenant with God," he told the *Times*. "As I see it, if a woman shares equally, it is not only permissible to devise an appropriate ceremony for entering the covenant, it is a religious obligation."

To outsiders, these may seem like mild deviations, but in the super-strict world of the ultra-Orthodox, changing prayers, inventing ceremonies, and praying alone are considered signs of dangerous freethinking. Even Chabad, despite its nonjudgmental attitude, doesn't really go along. In mid-2013, Rabbi Sholom Duchman, who heads the Chabad charity organization Colel Chabad, took Eckstein to visit the Ohel on the anniversary of the death of the Lubavitcher Rebbe. On the way, they fell into a discussion of solitary prayer. Eckstein explained his belief that a heartfelt session with God was worth more than going briskly through the motions with a minyan in a synagogue. Duchman conceded that even the great Hasidic mystics had wandered in nature to commune with the Almighty, but only after having davened with a proper quorum. "Nine of the greatest rabbis in the world can pray together and God doesn't hear them," he told Eckstein, "but if ten plumbers pray together, God can hear. That's the law." Eckstein didn't argue; he and Duchman were friends and colleagues. But he also didn't agree, at least not in his own case.

It was Rabbi Duchman who initiated the Chabad-Fellowship association in 2003, letting Eckstein know that Colel Chabad would be happy to accept Christian assistance. At first, Eckstein was wary. The memory of the humiliation he suffered at his daughter's bat mitzvah, held in a Chabad shul, was still vivid. But Duchman assured him that it had been an isolated incident. "Chabad is a franchise, not a corporation," he explained. "The rabbi there was acting on his own."

Not everyone in Chabad was enthusiastic about the partnership. "There were attacks on me from within the movement," Eckstein says. "Some people asked, Would the Rebbe have allowed this?" The senior Talmudic authorities of Chabad read Eckstein's books, discussed the case, (presumably) mulled over the economic advantages, and by majority vote, decided that Eckstein and his donors were kosher. This was in line with Chabad's pragmatism. Its annual telethons always feature Gentile celebrities, such as Jon Voight, Louis Gossett Jr., and Dennis Franz; Christian donations are more than welcome. Chabad is unwilling to publish the names of the rabbis who approved the relationship with the IFCJ, but once it was in, it was all in. In 2003, Eckstein was given the Chabad annual Leadership Award. He receives a lot of honors, but that one was special.

———

Eckstein's reception at the Moscow synagogue on Shabbat morning was special too—in fact, it was nothing short of grand. He received the third aliyah (chanting the blessing before the Torah reading), a high honor. He was also asked to lead the *musaf* service—which he sang in a mellifluous cantorial tenor—and to deliver the sermon on the weekly Torah portion, making it a Shabbat hat trick. This was more than acceptance; it was a warm public embrace. At the reception that followed the service, he was seated next to the chief rabbi of Russia, Berel Lazar, who toasted Eckstein's health with a double "*L'chaim*" (and an excellent single-malt Scotch). After the reception he hosted Eckstein and Joelle at a three-hour lunch at his home.

Approaching fifty, Lazar is a trim man who, unlike Eckstein, *looks* like a rabbi, with a long beard and wire-rimmed glasses. He is Chabad royalty, the son of one of the first shluchim, chosen by the Rebbe himself to revitalize Jewry in Italy. He was born and raised in Milan and educated at the Rabbinical College of America, Chabad's central yeshiva, in Morristown, New Jersey. In 1990, just as the Soviet Union was falling, he was dispatched to Moscow, in what was certainly Chabad's most critical posting. That same year, Yechiel Eckstein launched On Wings of Eagles.

There was no Jewish infrastructure in Russia when Lazar arrived. He was charged with creating one—synagogues, schools, kosher food supplies, religious burial societies—from scratch. Russian society was in turmoil. More than a million Jews were leaving, and many who stayed were afraid to come out of the closet. Lazar and his family were impoverished. His first son died of an infection that could have been cured in a less backward medical environment. He and his wife buried the boy in Israel and returned to their post in Moscow. Since then, they have had eleven children, all of whom are, or will become, shluchim. One of Lazar's dreams is to build a world-class Jewish hospital, along the lines of New York's Beth Israel, in Moscow. Lazar arranged for Eckstein to meet with a senior official in the Russian Ministry of Health. During the course of that meeting, Eckstein made it clear that if the project goes ahead, it will have his financial backing.

Eckstein also had a conference with the Russian minister of development, who Lazar described as a rising star in Russian politics. The Russian government had recently built the Jewish Museum and Tolerance Center in Moscow. President Putin, who has a close relationship with Rabbi Lazar, attended the opening ceremony and announced that he was donating a month's salary to the museum. The well-publicized act influenced a number of wealthy Russian Jews to make generous contributions of their own. A few months later, Lazar went to the capital for a ceremony to which Putin had invited him. Returning around sunset on a Friday, he was forced to walk home twenty miles from the Moscow airport to avoid desecrating the Sabbath. Chabad, which is famous for its public relations expertise, alerted the local media to the trek and let it be known that the chief rabbi considered it an honor to walk eight hours out of respect for the president.

The Russian government was already planning to build ten regional museums of tolerance, and Lazar asked Eckstein to put in a word for an eleventh, in the town of Birobidzhan, the capital of the notional Jewish Autonomous Region, near the Chinese border. Stalin had established the region in 1931, as a counterweight to Zionism, but it never really took off. Today, the Jewish community of Birobidzhan is about four thousand, some 10 percent of the total population. There are a few quaint touches—one of the main streets in town is named for Sholem Aleichem, there is an annual government-financed Yiddish festival, and a large public menorah is constructed during Hanukkah— but a museum in the middle of nowhere isn't likely to attract many visitors. In a meeting with the minister of development, Eckstein praised the government's plan for museums, but he didn't promise to support the Birobidzhan branch. A monument to the failure of Communism to wipe out Judaism in the USSR doesn't fall within the guidelines of Isaiah 58.

The Shaarei Tzedek center for the elderly, in Moscow, makes for a better fit. On a scalding Monday morning, Eckstein visited the center, which is run by Chabad using Fellowship funds. He was greeted by a red carpet, a huge bouquet of flowers, and a military brass band playing marches of welcome. At the entrance to the building, a modern edifice not far from the Kremlin, a banner hung: "On behalf of the hundreds of thousands of Jews in the CIS [Commonwealth of Independent States], we salute the Fellowship of Christians and Jews and bless its leader, Rabbi Eckstein." Suitably pleased and embarrassed by the reception, Eckstein tossed the band a mock salute as he hustled up the front stairs.

Eckstein toured the premises, starting with the cafeteria. He peppered his guide with practical questions: How much does it cost to heat and cool the place? What sort of food is served in the cafeteria? How many people are fed each day? At tables, he stopped to interrupt seniors who were eating lunch and ask more questions. "How long does it take you to get here from home? How many days a week do you eat here? What is the average meal? Is the food good? What do you most enjoy doing here? How can it be made better for you?"

When Eckstein entered the social hall, several hundred people were waiting for him. An acoustic guitar orchestra serenaded him with Israeli songs. There were seven female guitarists and one male—roughly the balance of genders in the audience; in Russia, women outlive men on average by more than a decade. Eckstein took the stage and sang some popular Hebrew songs. People in the audience sang along; these were tunes they had learned at the center over the years. But when Eckstein switched to a Yiddish folk song, there was silence. The Jews of Moscow, even the old ones, no longer speak Yiddish; in Ukraine, which is poorer and less assimilated, there are still some native speakers.

After his impromptu concert, Eckstein gave a short talk, through an interpreter. He asked if anyone was familiar with the rabbinical concept of *tikkun olam*—literally, fixing the world. No hands went up. Russian Jews of this generation have had no religious education to speak of. Eckstein explained that the Talmud commanded Jews to do whatever they can to perfect humanity while knowing they can never finish the job. He cited Mother Teresa as a model, and there were nods of approval; Mother Teresa is a familiar figure. "It is my privilege to represent the Christians in America who want to join with you in fixing the world," Eckstein said, picking up his guitar. He sang another Hebrew song from the struggle to free Soviet Jewry, pausing in the middle to shout out, "We won! We lived! Stalin, eat your heart out!" This got a big round of applause.

After the show, the Chabad emissaries invited people to line up for food packages. The previously polite crowd suddenly began pushing and shoving to the head of the line for plastic bags of groceries with the logo of the Fellowship printed on the sides. Eckstein had been scheduled to personally hand out the bags, but when he saw the mob scene he withdrew. "I hate this," he said. "The needs here are really huge, and there are so many Russian Jews who have succeeded in business, here and overseas. They should be taking care of their own parents and grandparents. But they are more likely to support charities in Israel than Russia. For them, Israel is an insurance policy."

Russia is a sweet place for Eckstein. Thanks to Chabad and the Joint Distribution Committee, his philanthropy is dispersed without requiring him to engage with his *bête noire*, management. He doesn't need to justify his ministry to evangelical critics who want him to support Christian mission activities, liberal American Jewish apparatchiks who disapprove of his conservative donors and their uncritical Zionism, snide members of the Tel Aviv chattering classes who deride his American accent and Dudley Do-Right sincerity, Israeli officials who treat him like an ATM, or Haredi rabbis who portray him as an idol-worshipping heretic. There are no staffers to supervise in Russia, no board of directors to placate, no unfiltered *schnorrers* to dodge. In 2011, he was named Man of the Year by the Federation of Jewish Communities, in a ceremony at the Kremlin. He sang "Let My People Go," and the audience cried. So did Eckstein.

Russia is also a place where he had one of the most affirming moments of his career. It came early in the life of the Fellowship, when he led a group of about forty Americans to what had once been the Pale of Settlement. There, in a small village, they met an elderly Holocaust survivor dressed in rags. His shack was unheated and his legs and feet were blue from the cold, but that, he said, was not his greatest problem. He had a heart condition that required an operation, and he couldn't afford one, so he had resigned himself to dying.

Eckstein chokes up when he talks about what happened next. "One of the men traveling with us, a Jew, asked how much it would cost. The old man said it was $500. The Jew took out his wallet, counted out $250, put it in the old man's hand, and said, 'You're halfway there.' Then one of the Christians took out his wallet, gave the old man the rest of the money, and said, 'Have the operation and may God bless you.' That, to me, is a moment that symbolizes what I have been trying to accomplish, Christians and Jews coming together to bless one another."

Fifteen

❖

REFLECTIONS

A few weeks after returning from Russia, Yechiel Eckstein decided to do something he had been putting off for twenty years. Accompanied by his daughter Talia and a friend from Israel, he returned to the Chicago Community Kollel in West Rogers Park, the scene of his greatest humiliation—the public declaration that he was unfit to be a Jew among his fellow Jews.

The Kollel is a small, low building on North California Avenue, in a neighborhood full of Orthodox shuls and schools. There was no one around when he entered, but a heavyset woman popped out of an office down the hall and asked how she could help him. Eckstein stood there for a long moment. "I used to learn here," he said, using the yeshiva term for studying.

The secretary peered at him without recognition.

"My name is Yechiel Eckstein," he said.

"Oh," she said, sounding flustered. "Oh, yes."

"I haven't been here in a long time," he said.

The woman nodded.

"I just want to look around."

"I'll have to call the rabbi," she said.

"No need to bother anyone." He cast a glance toward his old classroom. "The place still looks the same."

"Just wait here," the secretary said. "I'll call the rabbi. He'll be here in two minutes." She went into an office, leaving Eckstein standing in the foyer.

The secretary was right. Within two minutes a small man with a white beard, dressed in black, walked in through the back door, as if he had been waiting out there all these years. Eckstein blinked. It was his old teacher, the guy who suspended him from his studies.

The man approached, stopping two feet short of a handshake, and stared blankly at his visitor. His face showed no recognition.

"I don't know if you remember me," Eckstein said after an uncomfortable silence.

"I know who you are," said the teacher in an old-timey Brooklyn accent.

"Yechiel Eckstein," said Eckstein. "You were my teacher. It's good to see you again."

"Thank you," said the teacher. There was an awkward pause where "good to see you too," belonged.

Eckstein shifted his weight from one foot to the other. "How have you been?"

"Baruch Hashem [Praise God]," said the teacher.

"Baruch Hashem," Eckstein responded, although the teacher hadn't asked how he was. After another long silence Eckstein introduced his daughter and his Israeli friend. The teacher nodded with evident indifference.

"I haven't been here in twenty years," Eckstein said. "Do you remember?"

The teacher nodded. "There was a question about you. You were, uh, *questionable*."

"But you knew what I was doing," Eckstein said. "You and I discussed it. It wasn't a secret."

"That's true," said the teacher. "But what we discussed was discussed privately. When it got into the newspaper that you were studying here it became a question. And with a question, you have to have an answer."

"You could have ruined his life," the Israeli friend said. "He was almost excommunicated."

"It could have been handled better," said the teacher, without emotion. "Without the publicity."

"Have you followed Rabbi Eckstein's career?" asked the friend.

The teacher shrugged his shoulders. "I hear things," he said.

"He's done a lot for the Jewish people. Don't you think you owe him an apology?"

"As I said, it could have been handled better. But if there's a question . . ."

Talia's eyes were filling with tears. She was Daddy's little girl again, sitting on her father's lap at the dinner table protecting him from Bonnie's disapproval.

"What if Rabbi Eckstein wanted to come back here and learn again, in the Kollel. Would he be welcome?" asked the Israeli friend.

"That's a good question," said Eckstein. "How would you feel if I wanted to come back?"

"I'd have to consult with our rabbis," said the teacher, shrugging his narrow shoulders. "What can I do? You know, you're still questionable."

Talia burst into tears and ran out of the building. Eckstein followed her with his eyes but he didn't move. Twenty years had passed since what he calls "the incident" at the Kollel. Since then he had helped millions of Jews around the world, taught Christians how to support and care for Israel and the Jewish people, been an *Eckstein*—a cornerstone—of world Jewry. Psalm 118 describes how "the stone that the builders rejected has become the cornerstone . . . and it is marvelous in our eyes." But Eckstein wasn't marvelous in the eyes of his old teacher, and he never would be. It was a painful realization, but it was also a moment of liberation, one that found expression a few weeks later, on the Jewish New Year, at the Lake Shore synagogue.

Lake Shore is a small, modern Orthodox shul that draws its members from Chicago's Gold Coast and nearby Old Town, a haven for young professionals. For the past ten years, Eckstein has served as its rabbi on the High Holidays.

Normally Eckstein doesn't look forward to the job. "Prayer is extremely personal to me, and I find it almost impossible to pray with the proper intentionality and lead services at the same time," he says.

"But I think people get something out of it, so I just keep coming back." This year, though, he came with a message: The time had come for modern Orthodox Jews to stop ceding the moral high ground to reactionary, xenophobic ultra-Orthodox rabbis whose goal was to exclude anyone who didn't recognize their authority and to maintain antiquated practices at the expense of spiritual relevance.

"If we can't get rid of the *bracha* [blessing] of thanking G-d for not making us women, a *bracha* I have not recited for thirty years, we have a problem," he said. "And we should feel uncomfortable with prayers saying that we were exiled from the Land of Israel 'because of our sins.' After the Holocaust, the murder of more than a million innocent children, is it any longer possible to ascribe our suffering and persecution to our sins? Is this really what we feel comfortable affirming and praying?"

Eckstein was especially concerned about ultra-Orthodox control of Israeli rabbinical courts, which have jurisdiction over issues of personal status such as conversion and marriage. "Let me share with you the shocking extent of how broken and untenable the situation in Israel is today because of the influence of the Haredi Orthodox," he told his congregants. "There are over 300,000 Russian Israeli citizens who are not Halachically Jewish. And there are about 100,000 children of Russian immigrants born in Israel, with non-Jewish status. They will be drafted to the army when they reach eighteen, but they won't be allowed to marry in Israel." Nor could they convert to Judaism; the rabbinical courts of Israel make that so difficult that few Russian Jews even try.

"These are issues with which I struggle," Eckstein said. "They are personal matters, but they are also questions of Jewish survival."

It was Eckstein's intention to return to Israel after the holidays and join forces with the small band of politicians and liberal Orthodox rabbis who are seeking to reform the rabbinical courts and curtail their coercive power. He felt a responsibility to the disenfranchised Israelis he had helped bring to their new country. Besides, he confided to friends, he was feeling old and exhausted from his incessant travel. His heart condition was a constant concern. Fighting the entrenched rabbinical establishment in Israel would be arduous, but at least it could be done from the relative comfort of home.

The entrenched black-hat rabbinical establishment was well aware of Eckstein's sentiments, and it continued its efforts to portray him and his activities as unkosher. An example of its hostility surfaced not long after he got back to Jerusalem from Chicago.

At the behest of Israel's minister of education, Eckstein committed $10 million to funding a month of summer school and activities for Israel's poorest children, who otherwise would have spent the vacation roaming the streets. Dubbed "A Summer of Friendship," the initiative specifically left all matters of curriculum in the hands of the Department of Education; Eckstein would simply pay teachers and staff and fund outings to amusement parks.

News of the program leaked to the press, and all hell broke loose. Eckstein was trying to help Christians convert Jewish children! Something must be done to stop him. Three prominent clerics issued a formal ban, declaring that it is forbidden to accept any charity from Christian individuals or organizations they support. To buttress their point they quoted an ancient rabbinical aphorism: "We do not seek their honey and we do not seek their bee sting." It was better for Jewish children to miss a month of schooling than to take Eckstein's money. (In the end the issue became moot. Hamas began firing rockets and missiles at Israel in the early summer. During the ensuing war, summer camps and schools in most parts of the country were suspended.)

To these ultra-Orthodox reactionaries, like their counterparts in the United States, Eckstein was irredeemably "questionable." But for the rest of Israel's major Jewish philanthropies, Eckstein and his Fellowship were not questions, but the answer. Day after day, requests for aid streamed into his office. Everyone, it seemed, needed and wanted his help. It was not an exaggeration to say that he had become one of the most influential and powerful Jewish philanthropists in the world. The black hats could oppose him, but the leadership of the Jewish mainstream saw and appreciated what he and the Fellowship meant for the needy in Israel and the Jewish world.

This appreciation was demonstrated in the spring of 2014, when the Joint Distribution Committee, the most important international Jewish welfare organization, awarded Eckstein its most prestigious prize, the Raoul Wallenberg International Humanitarian Award for extraordinary service to the Jewish people. It is a very big honor, a mark of acceptance—the previous winner was Nobel laureate Elie

Wiesel—and Eckstein was thrilled to get it. The ceremony took place at the Knesset in Jerusalem. Members of the Joint's board of directors—the cream of mainstream Jewish philanthropic leadership—were in attendance. So were an influential and transpartisan array of Israeli leaders, starting with Prime Minister Benjamin Netanyahu and Isaac Herzog, leader of the parliamentary opposition. Guests from Chabad and Israel's Christian Arab community were in the audience. So was his friend Haim Saban, the American Israeli media mogul and donor to the Democratic Party, who is Eckstein's partner in supporting the Friends of the Israel Defense Forces. On the dais was Speaker of the Knesset Yuli Edelstein, a former Soviet refusenik whose presence recalled Eckstein's days as a student demonstrating for Russian aliyah in the streets of New York.

The auditorium was packed with friends and family. Sy and Belle Eckstein, now in their nineties and living in Jerusalem, were front row center, radiating pride in the son they once derided as a fanciful dreamer; these days Sy Eckstein hugs his son and brags to the world that Yechiel is the family's legacy and its gift to the Jewish world. Yechiel hugs back, glad for the reconciliation. Joelle was there with her parents, who had recently moved to Jerusalem from Spain. Her efforts to get Yechiel to relax and smell the roses (or at least notice them) were heroic but not entirely successful. That night they were scheduled to go to a performance of *The Nutcracker*. Eckstein, recalling his first ballet, back in his student days, joked that he would once again use the occasion to bone up on the rules for the kosher slaughtering of a bull.

After a short biographical film tribute, Eckstein came to the podium. He spoke emotionally about his own aliyah and the sense of personal completion it had given him. He thanked the Christian "sacrificial donors" of the Fellowship who made its philanthropy possible and recounted the many ways in which their generosity was aiding Jews around the world and in Israel, and he spoke movingly about the rabbis and pastors and teachers—many of them no longer alive—who had profoundly affected his thinking and his long career. "My twenty-five-year-old self would have been shocked to meet me today, shocked that I was able to believe in something this big and actually do it," he told a friend before the ceremony.

Eckstein's address has the sound of a valedictory. Notably, he didn't mention his future plans. His daughter Yael was in the audience; increasingly, he had been speaking of her as his successor. It was sweet for him to dream about slowing down, freeing himself from the pressures of daily life and constant travel. There were books he wanted to read, places to visit where he wouldn't be besieged with requests, hours he could spend with his wife and kids and grandchildren. There would be time, too, for the kind of davening he yearned for, moments of a transcendent feeling of oneness with the universe he had experienced as a young rabbi wrapped in his prayer shawl in the backyard of his home in Skokie.

It was a pleasant reverie, but it wouldn't last long. Eckstein's own temperament wouldn't allow him to stop, and he knew it. "I'd love to be able to take it easier," he says. "My wife and my doctors would appreciate it too. But there are needy Jews who need to be fed, Christians who can be reached with our message, whole communities that feel under threat. I'm like Michael Corleone in *The Godfather*. Every time I'm almost out, something calls me back."

He didn't know it, but a call was already on the way.

Epilogue

❖

"WHERE THERE ARE NO MEN . . ."

On May 16, 2014, at four in the morning, Yechiel Eckstein landed at the nearly deserted airport of Odessa, in the western part of Ukraine. He was met on the runway by three bearded rabbis dressed in black and a contingent of soldiers wearing tiger-striped uniforms and slinging AK-47 assault rifles. A pair of very large, very blond plainclothes officers hustled him into an empty security room, where a lone clerk stamped his passport. Then he exited directly to an armored SUV that waited with its engine running. A police car led the way through the city's streets, with two more behind the SUV. The caravan was met at the entrance to the Bristol Hotel by more soldiers and cops, who shepherded Eckstein through the ornate lobby and up to his room.

Once, before the Holocaust and the long rule of the Soviet Union, Odessa had been a major Jewish center, with some seventy synagogues.

Today there were just two, both headed by Israeli Orthodox rabbis. Both were on hand to greet Eckstein in the lobby when he came down in the morning, after a few hours of sleep. The rabbis were rivals, but mutual fear and need connected them now. Two weeks earlier, on May 2, street fighting had erupted in Odessa's downtown squares, pitting pro-government Ukrainians wearing orange armbands against pro-Russians wearing red ones. The Russian sympathizers took refuge in the Trade Unions House, which was set on fire. Some burned to death. Others died jumping out windows. A few who survived the fall were hacked to death by the mob.

Nobody knows precisely how many Jews live in Ukraine, once the heartland of European Jewry. After generations of Soviet antireligious pressure and intermarriage, a great many of the country's Jews are at best distantly connected to the Jewish communities in Odessa, Kiev, and Donetsk. There were assimilated Ukrainian Jews on both sides of the barricades, but the rabbis were mainly interested in staying out of the cross fire. In this part of the world, political volatility has traditionally been the occasion for pogroms and anti-Jewish mayhem.

Eckstein knew the rabbis of Ukraine well; for many years the Fellowship had been a mainstay of Jewish institutions there. They had been calling him with dire reports about the violence taking place around them, and their sense of abandonment. The US government had issued a travel advisory for the area, effectively ending contact with American Jewish organizations. The government of Israel, intent on maintaining good relations with Moscow, had been unresponsive. The rabbis begged Eckstein to come.

The soldiers and plainclothes cops were standing outside the Bristol Hotel when Eckstein and two local rabbis emerged and slid into an armored van. They drove downtown, disembarked, and began walking toward the trade union building. There were very few foreigners in Odessa, and his entourage of rabbis and security guards made the group more than a little conspicuous.

At the trade union building they found knots of mourners lighting candles or standing at quiet attention next to wreaths of red flowers. They stared at the rabbis. A Ukrainian journalist hired to conduct the tour assured Eckstein that the massacre had no anti-Semitic overtones, but as soon as he entered the burned-out building, he saw a large Star of David painted on a wall with a slogan in Russian underneath. Eckstein asked for a translation. "Death to the Jews," said the embarrassed journalist.

After his tour of the premises, Eckstein stationed himself directly in front of the Star of David, and spoke to the camera of his accompanying videographer. "People slaughter one another and it is the Jews' fault—always the Jews," he said. "This is our history. We have to build love and respect for one another. Otherwise, this sickness will just go on and on. We are grateful that there are Christians who stand with us and say, 'No more anti-Semitism.'"

Eckstein's gratitude was not misplaced. His donors responded with generosity. There would be enough money for whatever short-term contingencies he deemed necessary, in Odessa and throughout Ukraine. But he was also beginning to think about a longer-range solution.

On Saturday night, more than a thousand Jews gathered in the courtyard of the Chabad synagogue to celebrate the holiday of Lag B'Omer. A bonfire was lit, Hasidic music blared from speakers, vodka flowed, and men danced the hora. The young people gathered around, someone handed Eckstein a guitar, and he began to sing an Israeli folk tune. The kids knew the words and sang along. In their faces you could see a hundred years of assimilation and mixed ancestry, in their voices an easy familiarity with the Hebrew language. One of the kids was a dark-skinned seventeen-year-old soccer star, the son of an African father and a Jewish mother. Eckstein had met him earlier at the synagogue and learned that the boy was being scouted by Israeli teams.

What about all the others, he wondered, the ones who didn't excite the interest of professional teams in Israel? Most of the Jews had departed from Ukraine in the mass exodus of the 1990s, but there were untold thousands still there. If they were truly in danger, why should they settle for partial solutions? Why not join their brothers and sisters in Israel?

The answer became apparent six months later, on December 22, the sixth night of Hanukkah. An El Al charter landed at Ben Gurion Airport. On board were some 230 immigrants from Ukraine. The logo of the Fellowship was painted in large letters on the side of the plane.

Over the years, the International Fellowship of Christians and Jews had funneled almost $180 million to the Jewish Agency to help subsidize Jewish immigration. But the Agency—a pillar of the Zionist movement, once headed by David Ben-Gurion himself—was no longer focused on the mission of bringing Jews to Israel. This was ironic—the Agency's leader was Natan Sharansky, the most celebrated of all the Russian/Ukrainian Jewish refuseniks. But with the bulk of Soviet Jews evacuated, the Agency had shifted its focus to "Jewish identity" in the Diaspora, especially in the United States, where communities found themselves threatened by assimilation and intermarriage. It had neither the budget nor the energy to worry about the Jews of Ukraine.

And, as the civil war escalated, and reached eastern Ukraine, it became clear that there was something to worry about. In the cities of Luhansk and Donetsk, Jews became fearful of being caught in the cross fire or scapegoated by one or both sides. Economic instability made it hard for them to feed their families or maintain local Jewish institutions.

In September 2014, Eckstein returned to Ukraine to assess the situation. There had been no pogroms, but he encountered a pervasive sense of fear. The Jewish community felt alone and leaderless, unable to protect themselves or take care of their families. Eckstein saw himself as a protector of last resort. It was a role he was more than willing to fill. He had been raised on the ancient rabbinical precept "In a place where there are no men, strive to be a man." He looked around and realized that he would have to step up.

The first order of business was to establish a safe haven. The Fellowship had long supported a Chabad summer camp near the town of Zhitomir, west of the fighting. Eckstein provisioned it and told a few reliable local activists to spread the word that it was open to the Jews of the region.

At first, they arrived in small groups, by car or on buses that Eckstein supplied. As the fighting grew worse, the flow of people increased. And soon there were upward of two thousand in the camp, with more arriving daily. They came thinking that the camp would be simply a place to wait out the fighting and left most of their belongings at home; optimists didn't even bother bringing a winter coat. But as the situation grew even worse, an increasing number began to realize that they had no future in the cities of eastern Ukraine, no matter which side won. They had become refugees.

To Eckstein, this was obvious, and so was the solution: aliyah.

But it wasn't an easy sell. There had been a war in Gaza that summer, which made the gun-shy Ukrainians nervous. And most of them weren't really Zionists anyway. These were people who stayed behind.

Still, the idea of going to Israel wasn't entirely foreign. Many of them had relatives who had prospered in the Jewish state. They knew from calls and e-mails that Israel wasn't really dangerous and it had its advantages. It was a place where they could manage in Russian, the weather was wonderful, schools were good, and the government provided aid for housing and job retraining. Most important, Israel was a country eager for them to come. Getting a visa for someplace better would be difficult and time-consuming. To sweeten the deal, Eckstein offered them free airfare and a stipend of $1,000 for each adult and $500 per child, to help defray the initial cost of resettlement. People started signing up. Eckstein chartered a plane.

When the Jewish Agency heard about this, it protested that

Eckstein was infringing on its franchise. It demanded that he donate money as he had always done, and let the Agency handle the operation. But the Agency, as far as Eckstein could tell, was not ready, willing, or able to move quickly enough.

Eckstein said he would give the Agency money on two conditions: It had to make Ukrainian aliyah a serious priority, and it had to give public recognition of the fact that this aliyah was being paid for by Christian Zionists.

The Agency balked. Its leaders accused Eckstein of being a publicity hound. He was annoyed by this, but undeterred. The way he saw it, the Jewish Agency was failing to rise to an emergency or fulfill its mission. He denied that the recognition he sought was personal. He had simply decided he would no longer allow his Christian Zionist donors to be swept under the rug.

In October, Eckstein announced that the Fellowship would open its own independent aliyah operation. This was a bold move. The Jewish Agency is a pillar of the Israeli establishment. Sharansky was close to Prime Minister Netanyahu, and still a national hero. But Eckstein wasn't deterred. He no longer looked up to the leaders of Israel or put absolute trust in their judgment and competence. Time and exposure had made him a realist. He had built the Fellowship by taking on conventional wisdom and overcoming entrenched establishments. Here was another hurdle. He had no doubt he could clear it.

A week after the first Friendship flight landed in Tel Aviv, he brought another 230 immigrants on a second flight. The Zhitomir camp was still full, and Eckstein began scheduling more flights. How many more would depend on the situation in Ukraine. There are perhaps 200,000 people in Ukraine eligible for Israeli citizenship under the Law of Return, but Eckstein resolved to take any Jew requesting help. "I can do this," he assured associates. "We can raise whatever money is needed. God will bless the effort and our donors will be excited to help Jews in distress reach the Holy Land." Eckstein was excited too. He saw it as a chance to save Jewish lives, to help Israel and give purpose to his followers. Nor would the effort be limited to Ukraine. After the murder of Jews by Muslims at a kosher supermarket in Paris in January 2015, he began planning to expand his aliyah efforts to France and beyond.

Here was the culmination of his career. Over decades, he had built a bridge between Christians and Jews. It was a historic project, a span over two thousand years of enmity and misunderstanding. No one had believed that such a bridge could be built, but here it now stood, stretching around the world and leading to Jerusalem— a sturdy edifice made out of faith and fellowship, grand dreams and quotidian labor, optimism and unyielding determination, ready to carry multitudes on a journey home to Zion.

Index

❖